I0095806

BEYOND THE CHECKLIST

Raising Neurodivergent Teen
Girls with Confidence

NICCI BROCHARD
&
DR. BEN CHUBA

BEYOND THE CHECKLIST

Raising Neurodivergent Teen
Girls with Confidence

Copyright©2025

All rights reserved by Nicci Brochard and Dr. Ben Chuba

Published in the United States by Cross Border Publishers.

No part of this publication may be reproduced, stored, or transmitted in any form or by any means electronic, mechanical, photocopying, recording, or otherwise without prior written permission from the author or publisher, except for brief excerpts used in reviews or educational purposes as permitted by law.

This book is protected under U.S. and international copyright laws. Unauthorized reproduction, distribution, or adaptation of any portion of this work may result in legal consequences.

For permissions, licensing, or inquiries, please contact

info@crossborderpublishers.com: www.crossborderpublishers.com

Book Formatting by: *MoNish*

Book cover design by: *Billy Design*

CROSSBORDER
PUBLISHERS LLC

New York, London, Quebec

CONTENTS

Introduction

When we think about neurodivergence, the image that often comes to mind is not that of a teen girl, but rather of a young boy; energetic, talkative, perhaps a little too impulsive, and often misunderstood in classroom settings. This stereotype is deeply ingrained in society, and as a result, many neurodivergent girls, particularly those with conditions like autism spectrum disorder (ASD), attention deficit hyperactivity disorder (ADHD), and other neurodevelopmental differences, go unnoticed, underdiagnosed, or misdiagnosed. But these girls are there, quietly navigating the world in ways that often go unrecognized.

For many parents, educators, and even healthcare providers, understanding neurodivergent girls can be a challenge because of the way these traits manifest differently in girls compared to boys. Girls with ADHD may not display the classic hyperactive behaviors associated with the disorder. Instead, they may be quieter, more internal, or struggle with self-regulation in ways that aren't immediately obvious. Similarly, a girl with autism might mask her true feelings to fit in with her peers, masking the sensory overload or social confusion that she may experience. These subtle, often invisible struggles contribute to the fact that neurodivergent girls are frequently overlooked, leaving them feeling misunderstood or even isolated.

This book, *Beyond the Checklist: Raising Neurodivergent Teen Girls with Confidence*, aims to change that. It's time to acknowledge the uniqueness of neurodivergent girls and to celebrate their strengths and challenges. This is not just another parenting guide filled with checklists and strategies for managing symptoms; though practical advice is certainly part of the conversation. Instead, this book is about fostering confidence, empowerment, and understanding in both neurodivergent girls and the people who support them.

Dispelling Myths About Neurodivergent Girls

There is no shortage of misconceptions about neurodivergence, especially when it comes to girls. The most pervasive myth is that girls don't experience neurodevelopmental differences as profoundly as boys do. This belief is deeply flawed and contributes to the underdiagnosis and misunderstanding of neurodivergent girls. For example, many people believe that autism, ADHD, or other conditions manifest in the same way in girls as they do in boys. But the truth is, girls often present differently. While boys might struggle with impulsivity, hyperactivity, or visible behavioral issues, girls are more likely to internalize their experiences, leading to anxiety, depression, or social withdrawal. They may exhibit subtle signs, like withdrawing socially, becoming perfectionistic, or experiencing intense emotional highs and lows, which can be easily dismissed as typical teenage mood swings or attributed to "just being a girl."

Another common myth is that girls "grow out of it." The idea that neurodivergent traits are just phases that girls will outgrow fails to acknowledge that these traits are often lifelong, even though they may look different as a girl matures. As girls transition into their teenage years, their challenges may become more pronounced due to the increasing demands of school, social expectations, and changes in their bodies. What we often see are coping mechanisms that might work in the short term but fail to address the underlying needs. This book will show you how to recognize these signs and address them with the care and confidence that every neurodivergent girl deserves.

Why Girls Are Underdiagnosed or Misdiagnosed

Neurodivergence in girls is often overlooked or misdiagnosed because girls are socialized differently than boys and are expected to conform to different behavioral norms. Where boys may be encouraged to assert themselves or express their frustrations through active behavior, girls are often taught to be more controlled, to stay quiet, and to fit into the molds of social expectations. As a result, girls are less likely to exhibit the outwardly disruptive behaviors that would raise red flags for teachers, parents, and doctors. Instead, their neurodivergence may show up as anxiety, depression, or social withdrawal, which can often be misdiagnosed as a mental health issue rather than a neurodevelopmental difference.

Additionally, because neurodivergent girls tend to internalize their struggles, their behaviors may not be as noticeable to those around them. Many girls develop coping mechanisms, such as "masking," where they consciously suppress their neurodivergent traits in order to fit in socially. This can lead to frustration and burnout, as they constantly try to live up to societal expectations that don't match their true selves. It also means that girls can go undiagnosed until they hit adolescence, when the social and academic pressures intensify and their coping strategies break down.

What This Book Offers (Support, Strategy, and Confidence)

This book isn't just about understanding the neurodivergent brain; it's about understanding and supporting the individual girl behind the diagnosis. It's about giving parents, caregivers, educators, and even the girls themselves the tools they need to thrive in a world that may not always understand them. The journey toward self-acceptance and confidence is a nuanced and deeply personal one. And it's a journey that requires a combination of compassion, education, and practical strategies to help girls navigate the world in ways that make sense for them.

Throughout this book, you will find support in the form of real-world examples, actionable strategies, and guidance on how to help neurodivergent teen girls build confidence. This book offers a roadmap for understanding neurodivergence in girls and, perhaps more importantly, for fostering an environment where neurodivergent girls can thrive. You will find practical advice on helping girls develop life skills, social strategies, and coping mechanisms that work for them. But you will also find encouragement to embrace their unique strengths, to see the beauty in their way of thinking and interacting with the world, and to understand the importance of their voice and perspective.

In the chapters that follow, we will explore how to support neurodivergent teen girls as they navigate the challenges of adolescence, how to recognize their strengths, and how to guide them toward becoming self-advocates who are proud of who they are. This book is about empowerment; empowering both the girls and those who care for them to create a world where neurodivergence is understood, accepted, and celebrated.

This journey is one of growth; not just for the girls we care about but for all of us as we learn to support them, understand them, and ultimately, celebrate them for the beautiful, unique individuals they are.

Nicci and I (Ben) thank you immensely for choosing our book.

CHAPTER 1

Not Just a Boy Thing: Understanding Neurodivergence in Girls

———— ⧼⤫⧽ ————

When it comes to neurodivergence, many people still assume that conditions like ADHD and autism predominantly affect boys. This outdated perspective has led to widespread underdiagnosis and misdiagnosis of neurodivergent girls. The reality, however, is that neurodivergent traits are just as present in girls as they are in boys. The difference lies in how these traits manifest and how they are often overlooked or misunderstood.

In this chapter, we will explore how ADHD, autism, and other neurodivergences show up differently in girls, how the concept of "masking" and "camouflaging" can hide these traits, and why traditional checklists used in diagnosing neurodivergence often fail to capture the reality of neurodivergent girls' experiences.

How ADHD, Autism, and Other Neurodivergences Show Up Differently in Girls

Neurodivergence refers to a wide range of conditions that affect how the brain processes information. While ADHD, autism, and other neurodevelopmental disorders are commonly recognized, these conditions often present differently in girls than in boys. Understanding these differences is critical to properly identifying and supporting neurodivergent girls.

ADHD in Girls: A Quiet Struggle

Attention Deficit Hyperactivity Disorder (ADHD) is one of the most common neurodivergent conditions, yet it often goes undiagnosed in girls. ADHD is typically characterized by inattention, hyperactivity, and impulsivity. However, girls with ADHD may present in ways that are less disruptive than the stereotypical hyperactive boy, which leads to their behaviors being overlooked or misinterpreted.

Boys with ADHD may be outwardly hyperactive, talk excessively, and engage in disruptive behaviors. These symptoms are often more visible and can lead to early diagnosis. In contrast, girls with ADHD tend to have more internalized symptoms. They may daydream frequently, struggle with organization, forgetful tendencies, or have difficulty focusing in school. These traits are often dismissed as laziness, forgetfulness, or emotional immaturity, rather than being recognized as signs of ADHD.

Real-life example:

Consider Emily, a 13-year-old girl who has been struggling in school for years. Her teachers complain about her difficulty completing assignments on time, her tendency to zone out during lessons, and her disorganization. However, Emily is not disruptive in class, and her behavior is less noticeable than that of some of the boys. It wasn't until her parents noticed similar struggles at home—difficulty with time management, forgetfulness, and losing track of things—that they began to seek a diagnosis. The ADHD symptoms in girls can be more subtle, and when combined with social pressures, they often go unnoticed until later in life.

Autism in Girls: The Quiet Maskers

Autism Spectrum Disorder (ASD) is another condition that affects both boys and girls, but it often manifests differently in females. While boys with autism are more likely to show clear social communication difficulties, restrictive behaviors, and intense special interests, girls with autism often develop coping mechanisms that allow them to appear more socially adept than they actually are.

Girls with autism may be more likely to "mask" their symptoms in social settings. Masking refers to the practice of hiding or suppressing one's true behaviors and emotions in order to fit in with others. This can be especially difficult for girls, who are often socialized to be more relational and nurturing than boys. As a result, they might internalize the pressure to meet social expectations, even if it means sacrificing their own well-being.

For example, Sarah, a 16-year-old high school student, has always struggled with social interactions but has learned to "blend in" by mimicking the behaviors of her peers. She avoids eye contact but forces herself to engage in small talk, even though it leaves her feeling exhausted. She avoids talking about her special interests, such as her love of animals, because it's often met with disinterest or teasing. This constant masking leads to emotional burnout, anxiety, and a sense of disconnection from her true self.

Real-life example:

Sarah's case illustrates how girls with autism often mask their symptoms in a way that makes them appear socially competent, though they struggle internally. This masking can delay diagnosis until adolescence or adulthood, when the emotional strain becomes unbearable.

Other Neurodivergences in Girls: Anxiety, Sensory Sensitivities, and More

Beyond ADHD and autism, girls can also experience other neurodivergent conditions, such as sensory processing disorder (SPD), learning disabilities, and executive functioning difficulties. These conditions often overlap with ADHD or autism, complicating the diagnosis.

Sensory sensitivities are common in neurodivergent girls, particularly those with autism. They may experience overwhelming reactions to lights, sounds, textures, or smells. Girls might avoid certain clothes or environments due to sensory overload but struggle to articulate these needs. These sensitivities are often misunderstood as behavioral issues, making it harder for them to be addressed.

Additionally, girls with neurodivergent conditions often face heightened levels of anxiety. The pressure to fit in and meet societal expectations can lead to stress and burnout. Anxiety often co-occurs with ADHD and autism, but because girls may internalize these feelings, their struggles with mental health are often overlooked.

Masking, Camouflaging, and Missed Signs

One of the primary reasons that neurodivergent girls are underdiagnosed is the concept of "masking" or "camouflaging." Masking is the act of consciously or unconsciously hiding one's neurodivergent traits in order to fit in with others or avoid judgment. For girls, this masking often starts at a young age and becomes more pronounced as they enter adolescence.

The Emotional Cost of Masking

Masking is exhausting. For neurodivergent girls, the constant effort to fit in can lead to emotional exhaustion, anxiety, and depression. Many girls begin to feel that they are living a double life—one where they are constantly pretending to be someone they are not. This dissonance can lead to a lack of self-acceptance and a deep sense of isolation, as the girl begins to feel that her true self is incompatible with societal expectations.

Masking is often more prevalent in girls because of the societal pressure to be socially adept, gentle, and nurturing. Girls are often expected to conform to social norms that value empathy, cooperation, and communication—traits that neurodivergent girls may struggle with. As a result, they often become adept at camouflaging their differences, masking their symptoms, and masking their true feelings.

Real-life example:

Lily, a 15-year-old girl, has always struggled with social interactions. She finds it difficult to read social cues and often feels out of place in group settings. At home, she is more comfortable and expressive, but at school, she forces herself to engage in conversations and join group activities, even when it feels exhausting. Her friends never see the anxiety or sensory overload she experiences, and they view her as "shy" or "introverted," not realizing that she is masking her true self to avoid standing out.

The Consequences of Masking

While masking can help girls navigate social situations in the short term, it can have long-term consequences. Over time, the emotional toll of suppressing one's true identity can lead to mental health issues, including anxiety, depression, and self-doubt. Girls who mask their neurodivergent traits may develop an intense fear of being "found out" or judged by others, which can further exacerbate feelings of isolation.

In many cases, girls will continue to mask their symptoms well into adulthood, leading to difficulties in forming genuine relationships, maintaining a career, or even managing their own mental health. By the time they receive a diagnosis, they may already have years of emotional and psychological strain to address.

Why Traditional Checklists Often Fail

One of the major barriers to diagnosing neurodivergent girls is the reliance on traditional checklists or diagnostic criteria, which often fail to capture the subtle ways in which neurodivergent traits present in girls. Standardized diagnostic tools are often based on male-dominated models of neurodivergence, which focus on traits that are more common or visible in boys.

Gender Bias in Diagnostic Criteria

Diagnostic checklists for conditions like ADHD and autism tend to emphasize behaviors that are more frequently observed in boys, such as hyperactivity, impulsivity, or outwardly disruptive behavior. Girls, on the other hand, may not exhibit these outward behaviors and may instead struggle with internal symptoms like anxiety, depression, or difficulty with self-regulation.

In addition, girls tend to be more socialized to meet social norms and expectations, which can lead to an underreporting of behaviors that are often seen as problematic. For example, a girl with ADHD may be quieter in class and more prone to daydreaming, leading her teachers to assume she is just shy or uninterested in the material. Similarly, a girl with autism might struggle with eye contact or small talk but may not display the more visible, stereotypical behaviors of a boy on the spectrum.

The Need for Gender-Specific Approaches

To accurately diagnose neurodivergence in girls, it's essential to use diagnostic criteria that are more attuned to the unique ways in which girls experience and express neurodevelopmental differences. This requires clinicians and educators to take a more nuanced approach, one that considers how gender influences the presentation of symptoms.

Real-life example:

Olivia, a 12-year-old girl with autism, was often misdiagnosed with generalized anxiety disorder because her social struggles were viewed as shyness rather than the social difficulties associated with autism. Her parents finally sought a second opinion from a specialist who was experienced in diagnosing autism in girls. Through a comprehensive evaluation, they discovered that Olivia's difficulty with social interactions, sensory sensitivities, and preference for routine were all part of her autism spectrum disorder. This diagnosis allowed Olivia and her family to access the support they needed, but it wasn't until they sought a gender-informed approach that her needs were truly understood.

Conclusion

Understanding neurodivergence in girls requires a shift in both our perspective and diagnostic approach. The subtle ways in which ADHD, autism, and other neurodivergences show up in girls often go unnoticed due to traditional diagnostic criteria and societal expectations that prioritize boys' behaviors. The result is that girls are underdiagnosed, misdiagnosed, and often left to struggle alone.

By acknowledging the unique ways that neurodivergent traits manifest in girls, we can ensure that they receive the support they need. This support begins with recognizing the signs of masking, internalization, and subtle emotional struggles, and it continues through creating an environment where neurodivergent girls can be understood, accepted, and celebrated for who they are.

Understanding neurodivergence in girls is not just about diagnosis—it's about creating a world where they can thrive without hiding their true selves, where their differences are not seen as flaws, but as strengths. It's about recognizing that girls are just as neurodivergent as boys, and their experiences are just as valid.

CHAPTER 2

The Diagnosis Journey from Frustration to Clarity

The journey toward a neurodivergent diagnosis for your child, especially a teenage girl, is often filled with uncertainty, confusion, and an overwhelming sense of frustration. The signs are there, but for various reasons, they go unrecognized or misunderstood, often for years. Finally receiving a diagnosis can be a mixture of relief, anger, and, sometimes, grief, as the reality of what you and your child have been navigating finally comes into focus. Understanding what to expect before, during, and after the diagnosis, how to process your emotional responses as a parent, and how to communicate these diagnoses to your teen are all critical aspects of this complex journey.

In this chapter, we'll walk through what the diagnostic process looks like, the emotional rollercoaster that often accompanies it, and how to support both yourself and your child as you move forward with newfound clarity.

What to Expect Before, During, and After Diagnosis

Before the Diagnosis: The Long Road to Clarity

For many parents, the path to diagnosis starts with an intuition or a nagging sense that something isn't quite right. You may notice that your daughter struggles with things other kids seem to navigate effortlessly— like maintaining friendships, completing assignments on time, handling changes in routine, or dealing with sensory sensitivities. You might even have heard teachers or family members suggest that "she'll grow out of it" or that "she's just being a teenager." The problem, however, is that many neurodivergent traits, particularly in girls, can be subtle and masked by coping strategies or a more passive presentation of symptoms. As a result, these behaviors can be attributed to something else entirely, such as moodiness or social awkwardness.

For example, you might see your daughter struggle with staying organized, forgetting assignments, or failing to complete tasks—behaviors that might seem like typical teenage struggles at first glance. But deep down, you sense that it's more than just a phase. It's an ongoing pattern. Yet, it often takes time, persistence, and sometimes even multiple opinions from professionals before getting a solid diagnosis. In fact, girls are often diagnosed later than boys due to their ability to mask symptoms and internalize their struggles. As a parent, you may feel stuck in a waiting game—unsure of whether what you're observing is part of typical development or something more.

The Diagnostic Process: The Appointment and the Wait

Once you have the decision to pursue a diagnosis, the journey typically involves several steps. First, you'll seek a specialist—such as a pediatrician, psychologist, or psychiatrist—who has experience in diagnosing neurodivergence in girls. Depending on the region and healthcare system, this process can take weeks or even months.

In the early stages of the diagnostic journey, parents often complete questionnaires or checklists to provide detailed observations about their child's behavior. These forms might ask about your daughter's ability to maintain attention, navigate social interactions, and respond to changes in routine. Teachers, family members, and other caregivers might be asked to provide input as well. These observations are critical for building a full picture of your child's behavior, as neurodivergent traits often look different depending on the context (e.g., home vs. school).

The actual evaluation typically involves a series of interviews, behavioral observations, and standardized tests. For a comprehensive diagnosis, specialists often spend considerable time talking with both you and your child, collecting detailed background information, and conducting assessments that explore cognitive, emotional, and behavioral functioning. For some conditions like ADHD or autism, these evaluations can take several hours or even multiple sessions. It's not uncommon to feel nervous or anxious during this process, especially as a parent. You're looking for answers, but there's always the uncertainty of how things will turn out.

Real-Life Example: Megan's parents noticed that she was having difficulty making and maintaining friendships, was hyperfocused on certain subjects, and often seemed overwhelmed by sensory stimuli. After years of searching for answers and receiving inconsistent advice from teachers and doctors, Megan was finally referred to a specialist for an autism evaluation. The process involved multiple interviews with Megan and her parents, as well as detailed observations. After months of waiting and several diagnostic sessions, Megan was diagnosed with high-functioning autism. The relief was immense, but it also brought a flood of emotions that they hadn't anticipated.

After the Diagnosis: The New Normal

Once the diagnosis is made, the real work begins. You now have a clearer understanding of what your child is experiencing, and this can be a powerful tool for moving forward. However, the period after diagnosis is often one of intense emotion and adaptation. Many parents feel a sense of relief—finally, there is a name for the struggles your daughter has been facing. But there can also be feelings of grief, anger, and frustration as you come to terms with the fact that your child will face challenges that will require ongoing support.

It's important to recognize that receiving a diagnosis doesn't solve everything—it's just the beginning of a journey. There will be additional appointments, therapies, strategies, and accommodations to put in place. But with this clarity comes empowerment—the ability to advocate for your daughter, provide her with the tools she needs, and create a supportive environment where she can thrive.

Emotional Responses as a Parent: Guilt, Grief, Relief

Guilt: The "Could I Have Known Sooner?" Question

One of the most common emotional responses parents have after receiving a neurodivergent diagnosis is guilt. Many parents find themselves wondering if they should have recognized the signs earlier or if they somehow missed critical red flags. For parents of neurodivergent girls, this guilt can be amplified by the fact that girls often mask their symptoms and may not exhibit behaviors that are typically associated with the condition. The nature of neurodivergence in girls can make it harder to identify, especially when those around you, including professionals, may not fully understand how these conditions present in females.

It's essential to recognize that guilt serves no productive purpose in this situation. Understanding that your daughter's neurodivergence wasn't recognized earlier does not reflect a failure on your part. Rather, it reflects the broader societal and medical oversight of neurodivergent girls and the lack of resources and awareness that leads to delayed diagnoses. The guilt you feel is a natural part of the emotional journey, but it should be replaced by compassion for both yourself and your daughter as you embark on this new chapter together.

Grief: Mourning the "Expected" Life

Another emotion that parents may feel after diagnosis is grief. This grief is not about mourning the loss of your child, but about mourning the life you envisioned for her. Many parents come to terms with the fact that their child's path will be different from what they initially expected. It's normal to grieve the loss of milestones that may have been harder for your child to achieve—whether it's academic success, social acceptance, or independence. This grieving process is an essential part of coming to terms with the new reality, but it's important to remember that neurodivergence doesn't equate to limitation.

For example, when Emily's parents learned she had ADHD, they mourned the fact that their daughter might never fit into the traditional mold of academic excellence and social success. However, over time, they realized that Emily's unique strengths—her creativity, her enthusiasm, and her problem-solving abilities—were just as valuable as any conventional measure of success. Through support and understanding, Emily went on to thrive in her own way.

Relief: Clarity and the Path Forward

While guilt and grief can be overwhelming, relief is another common emotional response for parents after a diagnosis. Finally, you know what's going on with your child. The frustration of unanswered questions, missed diagnoses, and misinterpretations gives way to the clarity of understanding. Relief comes from knowing that you are no longer in the dark, and you have concrete information that can help guide your child's development.

This relief allows parents to embrace their role as advocates for their child. Armed with a diagnosis, parents can seek out the right therapies, educational accommodations, and support networks. It also provides a foundation for self-advocacy for the child, helping them understand their neurodivergence and equipping them with the tools they need to navigate a world that may not always understand them.

How to Explain Diagnoses to Your Teen

Explaining a neurodivergent diagnosis to your teen can be one of the most sensitive and important conversations you will have. Teenagers are at a stage where they are forming their own identity and grappling with self-esteem, and understanding that they are different in some ways can be a challenging revelation. However, handling this conversation with care, empathy, and positivity can make all the difference.

Start with Honesty and Clarity

When discussing a diagnosis with your teen, it's important to be honest but also sensitive. Avoid using negative language or framing the diagnosis in terms of deficits. Instead, emphasize that neurodivergence is a different way of thinking and processing the world, which comes with both strengths and challenges.

For example, instead of saying, "You have ADHD, and this is why you can't focus," try saying, "Your brain works in a unique way that makes it harder to stay focused for long periods. But you also have incredible energy and creativity that can help you succeed in many areas."

Focus on Strengths and Empowerment

As you explain the diagnosis, focus on your teen's strengths and talents. Help them understand that having a neurodivergent brain is not a limitation—it's a way of thinking that brings its own advantages. For example, many girls with ADHD are incredibly creative and can think outside the box, while many girls with autism have an intense focus on their passions, which can lead to remarkable expertise in certain areas.

Make it clear that being neurodivergent doesn't define them or limit their future potential. Instead, it means that they may face some challenges that others don't, but there are tools and strategies available to help them manage those challenges. Encourage your teen to view their diagnosis as a part of who they are—not as something to be ashamed of but as something to embrace.

Encourage Open Communication

Lastly, create a safe space for your teen to ask questions and express their feelings. This can be an emotional conversation, and your teen may need time to process the information. Encourage them to voice their concerns or fears and validate their emotions. It's crucial to let them know that it's okay to feel unsure or even upset about the diagnosis. Offering reassurance and understanding can help your teen feel supported as they navigate this new reality.

Conclusion

The journey to a neurodivergent diagnosis is a difficult, often emotional one. Parents may experience a range of feelings—guilt, grief, and relief—as they work through the process. However, the diagnosis itself offers clarity, empowering both parents and their children to move forward with confidence and understanding. For teens, being open and supportive about the diagnosis can help them accept their differences and find ways to thrive. With the right support, education, and communication, the diagnosis journey becomes one of growth, learning, and empowerment for both parents and their neurodivergent daughters.

CHAPTER 3

Rewriting the Rulebook Rethinking "Normal"

Raising a neurodivergent child—especially a neurodivergent teen girl—often requires a shift in perspective, not just for parents but for the child herself. Neurodivergent girls, whether they are living with ADHD, autism, or other neurodevelopmental differences, don't fit into the neat little boxes of traditional development. In fact, the very idea of a single, "normal" way to grow up, learn, and thrive needs to be reconsidered in the context of neurodiversity. Instead of seeing neurodivergent traits as something that needs to be fixed, parents can begin to embrace these differences as part of their child's unique strengths and capabilities.

In this chapter, we will explore how to embrace neurodiversity, let go of comparison-based parenting, and focus on celebrating strengths instead of constantly trying to "fix" challenges. This shift is fundamental not only for the well-being of neurodivergent children but also for creating a family dynamic built on respect, understanding, and pride in diversity.

Embracing Neurodiversity, Not Just Coping

Neurodiversity is the idea that neurological differences—such as autism, ADHD, dyslexia, and others—are a natural part of human diversity. The neurodiversity movement encourages us to recognize that these differences are not inherently "bad" or something to be "fixed," but instead are valuable perspectives that contribute to the richness of human experience.

For parents of neurodivergent teens, it can be easy to fall into the trap of thinking that their child's differences are something to be "coped with" or "overcome." While it's important to support your child in managing challenges, it's equally crucial to shift the focus from mere survival to embracing and nurturing their neurodivergent traits as unique attributes that contribute to their identity.

Real-Life Example: Take the example of Clara, a 14-year-old girl with ADHD. Clara's mother, Amanda, initially found herself frustrated as her daughter would often interrupt conversations, forget assignments, and struggle to stay on task at school. She worked tirelessly to "fix" Clara's behavior, seeking strategies that would make her more "normal" in the eyes of her teachers and peers. However, after seeking counseling and becoming involved in support groups for parents of neurodivergent children, Amanda realized that Clara's impulsivity and creativity were traits that could be nurtured, not suppressed. With this shift in perspective, Amanda began to focus on Clara's remarkable problem-solving abilities and creativity, traits that made her excel in fields like art and design.

Embracing neurodiversity doesn't mean ignoring your child's difficulties; it means recognizing and valuing what they bring to the table, regardless of whether they fit the conventional mold. Instead of viewing your child's neurodivergent traits as something that needs to be "fixed," you can celebrate them as part of their individuality and intrinsic value.

Letting Go of Comparison Parenting

In a world that constantly promotes comparison—whether it's about academic success, social milestones, or career paths—it's hard not to compare your child to others, especially when you're raising a neurodivergent teen who doesn't fit traditional societal expectations. Parents often feel pressure to measure their child's progress against the "normal" developmental timeline, whether it's comparing grades, social behavior, or the ability to make friends. But this approach is not only detrimental to your child's self-esteem, it also prevents you from appreciating the unique trajectory your child is on.

The desire to compare your child to others is natural, but it's important to understand that neurodivergent teens often face different challenges that make such comparisons not only unfair but also unproductive. Neurodivergent girls often develop at their own pace, face unique social hurdles, or excel in nontraditional ways. These differences don't reflect a lack of ability, but rather an alternative way of processing the world around them.

Real-Life Example: Lily, a 16-year-old with autism, had always been somewhat of an outlier in her school. While her peers seemed to effortlessly navigate friendships and school events, Lily often found herself overwhelmed by social interactions and had trouble making eye contact, which led to social misunderstandings. Her mother, Carla, initially tried to get Lily to "fit in" by encouraging her to engage in activities that made her uncomfortable. Carla's comparisons with her other daughter, who was more socially adept, only fueled her frustration and disappointment.

It wasn't until Carla stopped comparing Lily to her peers that she began to see her daughter's strengths in a new light. Lily was incredibly insightful about the world around her, had a strong sense of justice, and was particularly talented at problem-solving. Carla began to embrace these qualities, allowing Lily to focus on activities that suited her—like volunteering for causes she cared about, participating in one-on-one social situations, and developing a deep love of animals. Lily may not have been "normal" in the traditional sense, but she was thriving in her own way, and that was enough.

By letting go of comparison parenting, you allow your child to grow into their own version of success. Instead of fixating on how they measure up to their peers, you can encourage them to define success based on their values, strengths, and interests. This will allow them to build confidence in who they are rather than feeling inadequate because they don't fit a conventional standard.

Celebrating Strengths Over "Fixing" Challenges

As parents of neurodivergent children, there's often a temptation to focus on "fixing" challenges or weaknesses. This can mean pushing your child to meet academic standards, social norms, or behavioral expectations that may not align with their neurodivergent traits. While it's important to provide support and help them manage challenges, it's equally important to emphasize their strengths and foster an environment where they can thrive without the pressure to conform to societal norms.

Rather than fixating on what your teen "can't" do, celebrate what they can do. Help them identify their passions, their talents, and their unique gifts. Every neurodivergent teen has strengths—whether it's in creativity, empathy, problem-solving, or resilience. By nurturing these strengths, you give your child the tools to thrive in a world that may not always be accommodating to their differences.

Real-Life Example: Sophie, a 17-year-old with ADHD, had always struggled with time management and organization. Her parents tried various strategies, from planners to digital reminders, to help her keep up with her schoolwork and extracurricular activities. However, it wasn't until they shifted their focus to her strengths that Sophie began to feel empowered. Sophie had an innate ability to think outside the box and find creative solutions to problems. She was particularly good at brainstorming and collaborating in team settings. When her parents encouraged her to pursue a career in design, where these strengths would be highly valued, Sophie flourished. She began to see that her neurodivergence wasn't a hindrance—it was an asset in certain fields.

The key is to support your child in developing these strengths. Rather than focusing solely on areas of difficulty, provide them with opportunities to explore and hone their natural talents. Encourage them to pursue activities and hobbies that align with their strengths, whether it's art, music, writing, coding, or any other area where they excel.

The Power of Self-Acceptance and Advocacy

A significant aspect of celebrating your child's strengths is helping them to develop a sense of self-acceptance. Neurodivergent teens often face societal pressure to conform to a "normal" way of doing things, which can lead to frustration, anxiety, and a feeling of inadequacy. Encouraging your daughter to embrace her neurodivergence as part of her identity—rather than as something to overcome—can help her develop confidence and resilience.

Self-advocacy is a key component of this process. Teach your daughter how to communicate her needs and advocate for herself in school, at home, and in social settings. This will not only empower her but also help her build relationships based on mutual understanding and respect.

Real-Life Example: Madeline, a 15-year-old with sensory processing issues, had always been overwhelmed by noisy environments. In the past, her parents tried to "fix" this by pushing her to attend crowded events or ignoring her sensory needs. However, when Madeline learned how to communicate her needs—asking for a quiet space or noise-canceling headphones during stressful times—she gained more control over her environment. By advocating for herself, Madeline not only found ways to cope with her sensory sensitivities but also developed a sense of pride in her ability to stand up for her needs.

Conclusion

Raising a neurodivergent teen girl is about embracing a new way of thinking, both as a parent and as a family. It's about letting go of traditional standards of "normal" and creating a space where your child can thrive by celebrating their strengths and valuing their individuality. Instead of focusing on "fixing" their challenges, take the time to nurture their unique gifts, whether they lie in creativity, problem-solving, or empathy.

As you rewrite the rulebook of parenting, remember that neurodivergent traits are not deficits to overcome—they are differences that add depth, complexity, and beauty to your child's identity. By letting go of comparison, embracing neurodiversity, and celebrating your daughter's strengths, you empower her to navigate the world with confidence and authenticity. This is not just a path to growth for your teen; it is a path that will lead to a future where neurodivergence is seen as a strength, not a limitation.

CHAPTER 4

School Is Not Always Safe Navigating Education Systems

Education is often seen as a place for growth, socialization, and opportunity. However, for neurodivergent girls, the traditional education system can feel like an obstacle course—one that isn't designed to cater to their unique needs and abilities. In fact, many neurodivergent girls face significant challenges in educational environments, where their differences are frequently misunderstood, overlooked, or mishandled.

This chapter will explore how to advocate for your child's educational needs, including securing IEPs (Individualized Education Plans), 504 plans, and necessary accommodations. We'll delve into the common ways that schools fail to properly support neurodivergent girls and explore how you, as a parent, can collaborate with educators to ensure your child's dignity is preserved while meeting their needs.

Advocating for IEPs, 504s, and Accommodations

Understanding the Legal Framework: IEPs vs. 504 Plans

Navigating the educational system for neurodivergent children requires an understanding of the legal frameworks designed to provide support. The two primary avenues for securing support in U.S. schools are IEPs (Individualized Education Plans) and 504 Plans. Both of these plans are designed to provide accommodations to ensure that students with disabilities receive the support they need to succeed academically. However, they are distinct in their application and requirements.

1. IEPs: Individualized Education Plans

An IEP is a legally binding document that outlines specific educational goals, accommodations, and services that are required to support a child with a disability. It is designed for students whose disabilities significantly impact their ability to learn within a traditional classroom setting. In the case of neurodivergent girls, an IEP can help provide targeted interventions that address their specific needs, whether it's support for ADHD, autism, or other conditions.

For example, a neurodivergent girl with autism might need social skills training, a quiet space for sensory breaks, or modified assignments. An IEP ensures that these accommodations are legally required and that the school is accountable for providing them.

2. 504 Plans

A 504 Plan provides accommodations for students who have a disability but do not require specialized instruction. It is named after Section 504 of the Rehabilitation Act of 1973, which mandates that students with disabilities be provided equal access to education. While a 504 plan is not as detailed as an IEP, it can still provide essential accommodations like extended time for tests, preferential seating, or adjustments to class schedules.

For neurodivergent girls, a 504 plan might be appropriate if they don't require specialized teaching methods but still need adjustments to help them manage their unique challenges. This could include accommodations such as reduced homework load, frequent breaks, or support for executive functioning issues like organization and time management.

How to Advocate for Your Child's Needs

1. Know Your Rights

The first step in advocating for an IEP or 504 plan is understanding your legal rights and those of your child. The Individuals with Disabilities Education Act (IDEA) guarantees a free and appropriate education for children with disabilities, including those who are neurodivergent. This means that if your child's neurodivergent traits significantly impact her ability to learn, the school is legally obligated to provide support.

2. Document and Gather Evidence

Before seeking accommodations, it's crucial to document your child's challenges and the ways in which those challenges affect her education. This could include grades, teacher reports, behavioral observations, and any evaluations from healthcare professionals. This evidence will help you build a strong case for why your child needs additional support.

3. Request a Formal Evaluation

If your child is not already receiving services, you may need to formally request an evaluation. Schools are legally required to evaluate students who may need special education services, and this process should involve input from you, the teachers, and specialists. If the school refuses or delays the evaluation, you have the right to seek an independent evaluation.

4. Participate in Meetings and Negotiations

Once your child is evaluated, the school will hold an IEP or 504 meeting. This is a critical moment for you as a parent to advocate for your child's needs. Bring your documentation, ask questions, and ensure that the accommodations and services provided are appropriate and tailored to your child's needs. Remember, the school cannot simply offer generalized accommodations—it must be individualized.

5. Follow Up and Monitor Progress

After securing an IEP or 504 plan, it's important to regularly monitor your child's progress. Keep track of whether the accommodations are being implemented effectively, and be prepared to request adjustments if needed. Regular meetings with teachers and other school staff are essential to ensuring that your child is receiving the support they need.

How Schools Overlook or Mishandle Neurodivergent Girls

The Gender Bias in Diagnosing Neurodivergence

One of the reasons why neurodivergent girls are often overlooked or mishandled in schools is the gender bias in diagnosing neurodevelopmental conditions. While boys with ADHD, autism, or other conditions are often more easily recognized due to more overt behaviors like impulsivity or hyperactivity, girls tend to have more subtle symptoms. Girls are socialized to be more quiet, reserved, and compliant, which can make their struggles less noticeable.

For example, a girl with ADHD might exhibit quiet daydreaming in class rather than being disruptive, which may go unnoticed by teachers. Similarly, a girl with autism may avoid social interaction, but her social withdrawal may be attributed to shyness or introversion rather than a neurological difference. As a result, many neurodivergent girls are not referred for evaluations or do not receive the support they need.

The Challenges of Masking in Schools

Another factor that contributes to the mishandling of neurodivergent girls in schools is the tendency for girls to mask their symptoms. Masking refers to the act of consciously or unconsciously suppressing or hiding neurodivergent behaviors to fit in with societal expectations. Girls, especially during adolescence, are often under immense pressure to appear "normal" socially. They may learn to mimic social behaviors, such as making eye contact or engaging in small talk, even though these interactions are difficult for them.

While masking can allow girls to blend in temporarily, it often leads to exhaustion, emotional distress, and mental health issues. Moreover, because their struggles are hidden, educators and parents may not recognize the need for accommodations or interventions until the stress of masking becomes overwhelming.

Real-Life Example: Samantha, a 15-year-old girl with autism, learned to mask her social struggles by mimicking her peers. While she was able to avoid being openly ostracized, she struggled silently with feelings of isolation and anxiety. Teachers and classmates saw her as quiet but well-behaved, never realizing that Samantha was spending much of her energy pretending to be "normal." It wasn't until Samantha's anxiety escalated, and she began experiencing emotional breakdowns, that her neurodivergence was finally recognized.

Misunderstanding Behavioral Symptoms

Neurodivergent girls are also frequently misunderstood due to the way they express their behaviors. For example, girls with ADHD may show signs of inattentiveness and poor organization but may not display the hyperactive and disruptive traits typically associated with the disorder. Teachers might interpret this as laziness or lack of effort, rather than recognizing it as a symptom of ADHD.

Similarly, girls with autism may struggle with social communication, but this is often misread as shyness or introversion. These misinterpretations can lead to delays in intervention, inappropriate disciplinary measures, or feelings of alienation and frustration.

Collaborating with Educators While Protecting Your Child's Dignity

1. Building a Partnership with Teachers and School Staff

Collaboration with educators is essential to ensuring that your child's needs are met in the school setting. However, collaboration must be done in a way that respects your child's dignity and individuality. The relationship between parents and educators should be one of mutual respect and understanding, with the goal of creating a supportive, inclusive environment for the child.

2. Start with Empathy and Understanding

When approaching teachers and school staff, it's important to be empathetic and respectful of their position. Teachers are often overburdened, so it's crucial to approach them with understanding, while still being firm about your child's needs. Instead of framing your child's neurodivergence as a problem to be solved, approach the conversation as an opportunity to educate and work together for the best outcome.

3. Advocate, Don't Assume

While collaboration is essential, it's important not to assume that the school will automatically provide your child with the accommodations they need. Even with an IEP or 504 plan, there may be times when the school doesn't fully implement the plan or provide accommodations effectively. Be proactive in checking that accommodations are in place, and if they are not, don't hesitate to request changes or advocate for more tailored support.

4. Respecting Your Child's Privacy and Dignity

While advocating for your child's needs, it's also important to protect her dignity. Your child has a right to privacy, and discussing her neurodivergence with teachers and staff should be done with her best interests in mind. Encourage your child to be involved in the conversation and decision-making process when appropriate. For example, as your daughter matures, you may want to involve her in meetings with educators and help her practice self-advocacy skills.

Real-Life Example: Jennifer, the mother of a 16-year-old girl with ADHD, always made it a point to communicate openly with her daughter's teachers while respecting her privacy. When her daughter expressed discomfort with certain accommodations, Jennifer worked with the school to adjust the plan without making her feel singled out. This approach helped Jennifer maintain a strong, respectful relationship with both her daughter and her child's educators.

Conclusion

Navigating the education system for neurodivergent girls is complex, requiring parents to be persistent advocates while also protecting their child's dignity and well-being. Understanding the legal frameworks, building strong partnerships with educators, and recognizing the unique challenges faced by neurodivergent girls can make a world of difference. By embracing collaboration, understanding the nuances of neurodivergence, and advocating effectively, you ensure that your child not only survives but thrives in the school environment. The path forward is not just about making adjustments—it's about building a foundation of respect, understanding, and celebration of your child's strengths.

CHAPTER 5

Social Survival Friendships, Cliques, and Exclusion

———————— ⟨⟩✕⟨⟩ ————————

Navigating social dynamics is often one of the hardest aspects of life for neurodivergent teen girls. For many, understanding peer relationships, managing social anxiety, and dealing with exclusion are daily challenges that can significantly impact their self-esteem and emotional well-being. This chapter focuses on the nuances of social survival for neurodivergent teens, highlighting the importance of acknowledging social fatigue, helping them navigate friendships authentically, and offering practical tools like peer mentors and social scripts to ease the social journey.

Understanding Social Fatigue and Anxiety

Social interactions can be draining for neurodivergent girls, especially those who may struggle with conditions like autism or ADHD. Unlike their neurotypical peers, who often find socializing energizing, neurodivergent girls may experience social fatigue, a feeling of exhaustion from the constant effort to process social cues, engage in conversations, and maintain eye contact.

Social anxiety is another key component of the experience. The pressure to perform socially, meet the expectations of peers, and engage in group dynamics can lead to heightened stress and anxiety. Many neurodivergent girls face the added challenge of "masking," a process where they hide their true feelings and struggle to mimic neurotypical behaviors in social settings.

Real-Life Example:

Lena, a 14-year-old girl with autism, finds group socializing overwhelming. At school, she struggles to keep up with conversations, often missing social cues and feeling lost in larger groups. By the end of the day, Lena is physically and emotionally drained, but she doesn't know how to escape the pressure to "fit in" or the anxiety of being perceived as "weird" or "different."

Understanding and validating this **social fatigue** is essential. Parents and educators can help neurodivergent girls by acknowledging the need for regular breaks and self-care, as well as by advocating for environments where social expectations can be adapted to better suit their needs.

Helping Her Navigate Friendships Without Pushing Conformity

While neurodivergent girls may face difficulties in peer relationships, it is critical to foster authentic friendships based on mutual respect and understanding. It's tempting for parents to push their children toward conformity in a bid to help them "fit in." However, this approach often leads to frustration, anxiety, and a loss of self-identity.

Instead, focus on fostering genuine friendships. Encourage your daughter to connect with peers who share her interests and values. Helping her understand that not everyone needs to be her friend is important—healthy relationships come from mutual understanding, not forced conformity.

Real-Life Example:

Sophia, a 16-year-old with ADHD, often finds herself in conflict with her friends because she struggles to keep up with group plans or stays interested in a subject that others find boring. Her parents helped her identify one or two close friends who appreciated her spontaneity and unique perspective. These friendships allowed her to thrive socially, without the pressure of fitting into a larger, less supportive group.

Peer Mentors, Social Scripts, and Emotional Support

One of the most effective tools in helping neurodivergent girls navigate social relationships is the use of peer mentors and social scripts. Peer mentors are older or more socially experienced students who can guide and support your child through social interactions. These mentors model appropriate behavior, help with communication, and offer advice on how to handle complex social scenarios.

Social scripts are another helpful tool. These are pre-written scripts or guides that help the teen know what to say or how to respond in certain social situations. For example, a social script might outline how to greet a new person, how to express interest in someone's conversation, or how to exit a group discussion politely. These structured approaches help reduce anxiety and give your daughter the confidence to participate in social situations without the overwhelming pressure to perform.

Real-Life Example:

Maya, a 13-year-old girl with autism, was paired with a peer mentor in her school. Her mentor helped her understand how to initiate and maintain conversations, and over time, Maya grew more confident in her interactions. Through their regular sessions, she also learned how to use social scripts, which allowed her to navigate tricky situations like group discussions and parties with greater ease.

CHAPTER 6

The Executive Function Jungle Planning, Focus, and Chaos

———————$\gg\!\!\times\!\!\ll$———————

Executive function refers to the mental processes that help us manage our thoughts, actions, and emotions in order to achieve goals. These skills include planning, organization, time management, focus, and impulse control. For neurodivergent teen girls, particularly those with ADHD, executive function can be one of the most significant challenges they face in both academic and personal life. This chapter will address these specific challenges and provide strategies for helping neurodivergent girls build skills without feeling overwhelmed.

ADHD-Specific Challenges with Organization, Time, and Motivation

ADHD is perhaps the most well-known neurodivergent condition that affects executive function. Teen girls with ADHD often struggle with planning, staying organized, and managing their time effectively. Homework may pile up, tasks are frequently forgotten, and appointments are missed. Additionally, ADHD often brings issues with motivation, where a lack of interest in certain tasks (like schoolwork or household chores) can lead to procrastination.

Real-Life Example:

Olivia, a 15-year-old girl with ADHD, often forgets to turn in assignments or misses deadlines. She has trouble keeping her school materials organized and frequently gets sidetracked by distractions.

Despite her intelligence and creativity, her grades suffer due to her inability to focus or follow through on tasks.

Helping neurodivergent girls like Olivia requires understanding that these behaviors are not due to laziness but rather a challenge in executive functioning. Instead of reprimanding the behavior, we need to provide strategies and supports that work with the way their brains function.

How to Teach Scaffolding Without Micromanaging

Scaffolding refers to the process of providing support to help a child achieve a goal or complete a task that they may not be able to do independently. For neurodivergent teens, scaffolding can involve breaking tasks into manageable steps, using visual aids or checklists, and providing frequent reminders. The key is to support without overwhelming or micromanaging.

Instead of doing tasks for your teen, offer gentle guidance that allows them to build independence while still receiving support. For instance, if your daughter struggles with organizing her schoolwork, help her create a simple organizational system that works for her—whether it's color-coded folders, digital apps, or weekly planners. These tools should empower her to take responsibility without the frustration of trying to figure out the system on her own.

Real-Life Example:

Isla, a 16-year-old with ADHD, struggles to organize her homework assignments. Her mother helped her set up a digital calendar where Isla could break down assignments into smaller tasks with due dates. Over time, Isla learned to check the calendar independently and to make her own reminders. This scaffolded support helped Isla become more organized without feeling micromanaged by her parents.

Tools, Apps, and Strategies that Work With—Not Against—Her Brain

Technology can be a powerful tool in supporting executive function challenges. There are several apps and digital tools that can help neurodivergent teens stay organized, manage time, and focus. Apps like Trello, Google Keep, Forest, and Focus Booster can help with task management, setting reminders, and limiting distractions.

In addition to digital tools, consider other strategies like visual schedules, timers, and step-by-step guides to help with organization and task completion. These tools are designed to work with the brain's natural tendencies rather than against them, helping your child to succeed in a way that feels empowering.

Real-Life Example:

Mia, a 14-year-old with ADHD, uses the app Forest to stay focused while doing her homework. The app helps her set time limits for studying and rewards her with a virtual tree when she stays focused for a set amount of time. This system not only helps Mia stay on task but also creates a sense of accomplishment and motivation to keep working.

Emotions on Fire Meltdowns, Shutdowns, and Self-Regulation

Neurodivergent teens, particularly girls with autism or ADHD, often experience intense emotional reactions that can lead to meltdowns, shutdowns, or other emotional dysregulation. These responses are a natural part of navigating overwhelming stimuli, social expectations, and the emotional landscape of adolescence. This chapter will explore the hidden world of internal emotional storms, how to teach emotional literacy without shame, and how to support self-regulation through co-regulation and sensory strategies.

The Hidden World of Internal Storms

Neurodivergent girls often have emotional experiences that are heightened due to sensory overload, social misunderstandings, or difficulty managing internal emotions. For some, this can lead to meltdowns (intense outbursts of emotion) or shutdowns (a retreat into isolation and emotional numbness).

For girls with autism, sensory sensitivities can exacerbate emotional dysregulation. An uncomfortable texture on their clothes, a loud noise in the classroom, or a strong smell in the hallway can trigger overwhelming feelings of frustration and anxiety, which may culminate in a meltdown.

Real-Life Example:

Ava, a 13-year-old girl with autism, often experiences meltdowns when she is faced with sensory overload, such as loud environments or crowded spaces. At school, the sound of the bell ringing or the fluorescent lights can set off a wave of anxiety, which she struggles to manage. During a meltdown, Ava can't always communicate what's wrong, leading to feelings of frustration for herself and her teachers.

Teaching Emotional Literacy Without Shame

Emotional literacy is the ability to recognize, understand, and manage one's emotions. Teaching emotional literacy to neurodivergent teens involves helping them understand the different emotions they experience and giving them the language to express those emotions in a healthy way. This can be particularly difficult for neurodivergent girls who may already feel misunderstood or ashamed of their emotional reactions.

Instead of focusing on suppressing emotions, focus on acknowledging and validating them. It's important to create a safe space where your daughter feels comfortable expressing herself without fear of judgment. This means teaching her that emotions, whether positive or negative, are natural and valid.

Real-Life Example:

Lily, a 15-year-old with ADHD, often experiences frustration during school tasks when she struggles to stay focused. Her mother has worked with Lily to help her recognize when she's getting overwhelmed and to use simple self-calming techniques, such as deep breathing or taking a short break. Lily now feels empowered to communicate her emotions rather than suppress them, leading to fewer meltdowns.

Co-Regulation, Sensory Strategies, and Safe Space Building

Co-regulation refers to the process where another person (often a parent or teacher) helps a neurodivergent teen calm down during an emotional storm. This can involve guiding the child through grounding exercises, offering comfort, or simply being present without judgment. Over time, the goal is for the teen to develop the ability to self-regulate, but co-regulation is often a necessary first step.

In addition to co-regulation, sensory strategies can play a vital role in managing emotional overwhelm. These strategies can include sensory tools like weighted blankets, fidget toys, noise-canceling headphones, or creating quiet spaces where the child can retreat when they're feeling overstimulated.

Real-Life Example:

Jessica, a 16-year-old girl with autism, uses a weighted blanket and listens to calming music during moments of anxiety. When she feels herself getting overwhelmed, she knows to retreat to her quiet space and use these tools to help her self-regulate. Her parents have worked with her to understand her sensory needs and provide the tools she needs to manage emotions before they escalate.

Conclusion

Navigating the emotional and social challenges of neurodivergent adolescence is no small feat. However, by embracing your child's neurodivergence and providing the right support, tools, and strategies, you can empower her to thrive emotionally, socially, and academically. Understanding emotional dysregulation, fostering emotional literacy, and implementing strategies like co-regulation and sensory tools can help your child manage meltdowns and shutdowns. Likewise, supporting executive function challenges through scaffolding, organizational tools, and empathetic guidance will ensure she feels empowered to manage the chaos of life without becoming overwhelmed. Together, these strategies help build a foundation of confidence, resilience, and emotional well-being, paving the way for your neurodivergent teen to succeed in a world that may not always understand her unique needs.

CHAPTER 8

Body, Identity, and Sensory Worlds

———— ⧓ ————

Puberty is a tumultuous time for any teen, but for neurodivergent girls, the changes that occur during this developmental phase can feel even more overwhelming. Not only do they face the usual challenges of growing up; navigating changing bodies, hormones, and evolving social expectations but they also have to manage sensory sensitivities, body awareness, and a heightened emotional response to their rapidly changing physical world. For neurodivergent teens, sensory sensitivities can become more pronounced during puberty, and this can significantly impact how they experience their own bodies and interact with the world around them.

This chapter explores how puberty affects sensory sensitivities, navigating body awareness, hygiene, clothing, and self-image, and the importance of helping neurodivergent girls build body autonomy and acceptance. By focusing on understanding sensory sensitivities, encouraging healthy self-care habits, and creating a space of non-judgmental acceptance, we can help our daughters navigate this critical stage of development with confidence and self-awareness.

Sensory Sensitivities and Puberty Complications

The Intersection of Puberty and Sensory Sensitivities

Puberty is a time of significant physical, emotional, and hormonal changes. For neurodivergent girls, particularly those with autism or sensory processing disorders, these changes can be intensified by sensory sensitivities. Hormonal fluctuations can increase sensitivity to light, sound, touch, and other sensory stimuli, which can make familiar experiences seem more overwhelming or uncomfortable.

For example, changes in skin, hair, and body odor during puberty may lead to heightened awareness of tactile sensations. Clothes that were once comfortable may now feel itchy or constricting, certain fabrics might feel unbearable, and even basic activities like showering or brushing hair may become overwhelming due to sensory overload.

Real-Life Example:

Grace, a 14-year-old girl with autism, found that during puberty, her sensitivity to clothing textures became much more intense. She used to wear regular cotton shirts and jeans without issue, but as she went through puberty, these same fabrics started to feel itchy and unbearable against her skin. This change left Grace frustrated, as she had always prided herself on her independence in choosing her clothes. Her parents noticed that Grace was becoming withdrawn and self-conscious about her clothing, which led to long periods of wearing loose, oversized clothes that didn't aggravate her sensory sensitivities.

How Puberty Exacerbates Sensory Issues

Puberty brings an influx of hormonal changes, which can affect how the body responds to sensory stimuli. For example, a girl's sense of smell, touch, and taste might become heightened or altered due to hormonal changes. These fluctuations can make it difficult for neurodivergent girls to cope with new sensations in their environment.

Increased sweating during puberty, for example, can make the smell of body odor more intense. For a neurodivergent teen, who may already have heightened sensory sensitivities, this could lead to a strong aversion to the idea of body hygiene and self-care, potentially exacerbating feelings of discomfort, self-consciousness, and anxiety.

Additionally, the onset of menstruation can introduce new sensory challenges. The feeling of wearing pads, tampons, or menstrual cups can be uncomfortable, and the changes in body odor, texture, and the sensations of menstruation itself can be overwhelming. These challenges require empathy, patience, and strategies to help neurodivergent girls manage sensory overload during this phase.

Strategies for Managing Sensory Sensitivities During Puberty

1. **Sensory-Friendly Clothing**: Introduce clothing options that are comfortable and less irritating to the skin. For girls who are sensitive to fabrics, soft materials like cotton, seamless designs, or clothing without tags can be helpful. Consider layering, so they have more control over how much skin is exposed to different textures.

2. **Establishing Hygiene Routines Gradually**: Help your child develop a personal hygiene routine that respects their sensory needs. For instance, starting with a short shower in lukewarm water instead of hot water, or using fragrance-free soaps and lotions, can reduce sensory overload. If they struggle with brushing hair, try using detangling spray and a wide-tooth comb or consider scheduling a sensory break during grooming.

3. **Period Preparation**: Be proactive in preparing for menstruation. Consider offering a variety of products (pads, tampons, menstrual cups) and allow your daughter to experiment with what feels most comfortable. Introducing a menstrual calendar app or visual aids can also help with self-awareness, making her feel more in control of the changes her body is experiencing.

Navigating Hygiene, Clothing, and Body Awareness Without Judgment

Hygiene Challenges During Puberty

Puberty introduces new physical and emotional experiences that can be overwhelming, particularly when it comes to hygiene. As neurodivergent girls struggle with sensory sensitivities, the tasks of daily hygiene—like brushing teeth, washing hair, or using deodorant—can become daunting or unpleasant. For many, the sensation of water, soap, or even the feeling of a toothbrush in the mouth may trigger anxiety or discomfort.

It's essential to approach hygiene with patience and understanding, allowing your child to go at their own pace without making them feel ashamed or pressured. Encouraging small steps, offering sensory-friendly products, and creating a structured routine can help reduce the feeling of being overwhelmed.

Real-Life Example:

Sophia, a 15-year-old with ADHD, hated the sensation of shampoo in her hair and would often avoid showering altogether, preferring to stay in her room rather than face the discomfort. Her mother worked with her to find a shampoo that felt gentler on her scalp and allowed Sophia to shower in smaller increments, eventually building up to a more regular hygiene routine. By providing choices and reducing sensory discomfort, Sophia gradually became more comfortable with her hygiene routine.

Clothing Challenges and Body Sensitivity

As puberty brings about significant changes to a teen's body shape and size, it can create discomfort in clothing choices. Neurodivergent teens, especially those with heightened tactile sensitivities, may experience the sensation of wearing clothes as overwhelming, triggering a sense of frustration or anxiety. The pressure of conforming to social expectations around appearance and "fashion" can exacerbate these struggles.

Real-Life Example:

Emma, a 14-year-old girl with autism, struggled with wearing clothing that fit her body properly after she began experiencing growth spurts. She was self-conscious about her appearance and sensitive to the feeling of clothes against her skin. Instead of forcing Emma into popular styles or clothing she felt uncomfortable in, her parents provided her with options that prioritized comfort over fashion, such as stretchy leggings and oversized shirts, which helped Emma feel more at ease.

Building body awareness and self-acceptance is key. Instead of focusing on external appearance, encourage your daughter to appreciate the functionality and comfort of clothing that works for her. Provide a space where she can experiment with different fabrics, styles, and fits without the pressure of meeting societal standards.

Helping Her Build Body Autonomy and Acceptance

The Importance of Body Autonomy

As neurodivergent girls go through puberty, they need to learn about body autonomy; the right to control their own bodies and make choices about how they want to express themselves. Body autonomy is crucial not only for physical well-being but also for emotional health, as it helps girls develop a sense of ownership over their bodies, their needs, and their personal boundaries.

Helping your daughter understand body autonomy means respecting her right to make choices about her body and empowering her to express discomfort or preferences. Encourage her to make decisions regarding clothing, grooming, and hygiene based on what feels comfortable, and support her in understanding bodily changes like menstruation, breast development, and growth spurts.

Real-Life Example:

When Clara, a 16-year-old girl with ADHD, began developing physically during puberty, she struggled to accept her changing body. She felt embarrassed by her developing breasts and wanted to hide them with baggy clothes. Her mother gently guided Clara through the process of understanding body autonomy, encouraging her to try on different types of bras and clothing that could help her feel comfortable and confident in her own skin. Over time, Clara began to embrace her body's changes, learning to take ownership of her choices and expressing her comfort with more confidence.

Promoting Body Acceptance

Body acceptance during puberty can be a sensitive topic for neurodivergent girls, especially in a society that often emphasizes the "ideal" body. Helping your daughter develop a healthy relationship with her body involves challenging societal norms around appearance and encouraging her to appreciate her body's capabilities, rather than its outward appearance. Acknowledge her feelings, validate her experiences, and encourage her to express gratitude for her body's functionality and uniqueness.

It's essential to have open, non-judgmental conversations about body image. Offer reassurance that it's normal to feel uncertain about body changes and that everyone experiences puberty differently. Foster a culture of self-compassion and self-care, and help your daughter recognize the strength and beauty in her individuality.

Real-Life Example:

Jenna, a 17-year-old with autism, was struggling with body image issues and feeling out of place as her body changed. Her mother, recognizing Jenna's discomfort, created a safe space to talk openly about how she felt. Instead of focusing on societal beauty standards, they discussed Jenna's achievements, hobbies, and the qualities she loved about herself. This approach helped Jenna shift her focus from her appearance to her intrinsic qualities and the things she valued about herself.

Conclusion

Puberty is a time of significant change, and for neurodivergent girls, these changes can feel overwhelming and difficult to manage. By focusing on sensory sensitivities, body awareness, and hygiene practices, and by fostering body autonomy and acceptance, parents and caregivers can provide the support needed for girls to navigate this challenging phase with confidence. Through understanding, patience, and respect, we can help our neurodivergent daughters build a positive relationship with their bodies, feel empowered in their choices, and embrace the changes they are experiencing without judgment. This approach not only helps them during puberty but sets the foundation for a lifetime of self-acceptance, self-care, and body autonomy.

CHAPTER 9

The Quiet Crisis Mental Health and Masking

———— ⋈ ————

For neurodivergent girls, the process of **masking**—the act of hiding or suppressing one's true neurodivergent traits in order to fit into societal or social expectations—can be both an effective survival strategy and a silent crisis. While masking can help them navigate environments that might otherwise be overwhelming, it comes at a significant cost to their mental health. In this chapter, we will explore the link between masking and anxiety/depression, how to spot signs of burnout and shutdown, and how to support self-care, therapy, and healthy boundaries for neurodivergent girls.

The Link Between Masking and Anxiety/Depression

Understanding Masking: The Hidden Struggle

Masking refers to the conscious or unconscious effort to hide one's true behaviors, emotions, and traits to appear more "typical" or socially acceptable. For neurodivergent girls, masking is often a response to social pressures, particularly in environments like school or family life, where there are high expectations for conformity. Unlike boys, who may display more overt behaviors associated with ADHD or autism (e.g., impulsivity, hyperactivity), girls tend to internalize their neurodivergent traits. As a result, they may force themselves to conform to social expectations, leading to feelings of isolation, confusion, and frustration.

While masking can allow neurodivergent girls to fit in and avoid negative social consequences, it can also lead to significant emotional and psychological distress. The emotional toll of constantly suppressing one's authentic self contributes to feelings of anxiety and depression. The effort to maintain a "normal" facade can drain emotional resources and leave little room for self-care or self-expression.

Real-Life Example:

Sophie, a 15-year-old girl with autism, spent years masking her social challenges in order to fit in at school. She learned to mimic the behaviors of her peers, participating in conversations even though she didn't always understand the nuances. Sophie felt exhausted after each day, but she didn't know how to explain the overwhelming toll it was taking on her. Over time, she began to experience symptoms of anxiety—racing thoughts, worry about social situations, and a constant sense of being "on edge." She also began to show signs of depression, withdrawing from activities she once enjoyed and feeling hopeless about the future.

The Emotional and Psychological Impact of Masking

The psychological toll of masking is profound. Neurodivergent girls, particularly those who are forced to conceal their true selves in order to fit in, are at a higher risk for developing anxiety, depression, and other mental health issues. Masking leads to the following emotional and psychological consequences:

1. **Chronic Anxiety**: The pressure of always being "on" can create a heightened sense of anxiety. Neurodivergent girls might worry about making a mistake, saying the wrong thing, or failing to meet social expectations. This anxiety can become pervasive and interfere with everyday functioning.

2. **Depression**: The constant effort to fit in and suppress one's natural tendencies can lead to feelings of hopelessness and sadness. A neurodivergent girl may feel as though she is never truly understood or accepted, which can lead to a deep sense of loneliness and disconnection.

The Quiet Crisis Mental Health and Masking | 50

3. **Identity Crisis**: Masking can create confusion about one's identity. When a neurodivergent girl spends so much energy pretending to be something she's not, she may begin to lose touch with who she really is. This disconnection from her authentic self can lead to feelings of inadequacy, low self-esteem, and difficulty forming genuine relationships.

4. **Social Exhaustion**: Constantly managing and maintaining a "mask" is mentally and physically exhausting. Over time, the emotional and mental toll of masking can lead to burnout, where the individual no longer has the energy to continue masking and begins to disengage from social interactions altogether.

Spotting Signs of Burnout and Shutdown

Understanding Burnout: When the Mask Can No Longer Be Worn

Burnout is a state of physical, emotional, and mental exhaustion caused by prolonged stress or the continuous need to perform at an unsustainable level. For neurodivergent girls, burnout can happen when they have been masking their behaviors for an extended period, attempting to conform to external expectations at the expense of their well-being.

Signs of burnout include:

- **Emotional Exhaustion**: The individual feels drained, overwhelmed, and unable to keep up with daily demands. They may express feeling "tired of pretending."

- **Cognitive Overload**: Burnout can lead to difficulties with focus, memory, and decision-making. Neurodivergent teens may struggle to complete tasks that once seemed manageable.

- **Social Withdrawal**: After prolonged masking, a neurodivergent girl may withdraw from social situations to recharge or because social interaction has become too taxing.

- **Physical Symptoms**: Burnout often manifests physically through headaches, stomach issues, sleep disturbances, and fatigue.

Real-Life Example:

Lily, a 16-year-old with ADHD, had been masking her symptoms for years. At school, she put on a smile, forced herself to pay attention, and tried to keep up with her peers. Over time, Lily began to feel more exhausted and less able to concentrate. She started isolating herself from friends and family, feeling that she could no longer keep up the façade. Eventually, Lily's anxiety skyrocketed, and she experienced panic attacks, which led her parents to seek professional help.

Shutdowns: Emotional Withdrawal and Disengagement

In addition to burnout, neurodivergent teens may also experience **shutdowns**, which are emotional withdrawals in response to overwhelming stress. A shutdown often occurs when a teen has reached the limit of their ability to cope with sensory, social, or emotional stimuli. During a shutdown, the teen may retreat inwardly, withdrawing from social interactions and appearing "numb" or unresponsive.

Signs of a shutdown include:

- **Complete Emotional Withdrawal**: The teen may become non-verbal, avoid eye contact, or become physically distant from others.
- **Sensory Sensitivity**: The teen may become acutely sensitive to sounds, lights, or textures, reacting by shutting down or seeking out a quiet, isolated space.
- **Loss of Motivation**: During a shutdown, the teen may lose interest in activities they usually enjoy and appear emotionally distant or disconnected from their environment.

Real-Life Example:

Rachel, a 17-year-old with autism, often faced shutdowns during high-stress moments, like exams or large social events. During one such shutdown, Rachel retreated to a quiet corner in the classroom, avoiding her classmates and teacher. She couldn't explain what had triggered the shutdown, but she felt completely overwhelmed by the noise and pressure around her. It took Rachel several hours to recover, during which time she felt emotionally numb and drained.

Supporting Self-Care, Therapy, and Healthy Boundaries

The Importance of Self-Care in Managing Masking and Burnout

Self-care is critical for neurodivergent teens who are masking, as it allows them to replenish their emotional and mental resources. Teaching your daughter to recognize the need for self-care and giving her the tools to take care of herself are essential steps in reducing the negative impacts of masking and burnout.

Key aspects of self-care for neurodivergent teens include:

- **Rest and Recuperation**: Regular breaks and downtime are crucial for emotional recovery. Neurodivergent teens should be encouraged to take breaks when they feel overwhelmed, even if it's just for a few minutes.

- **Physical Care**: Promoting physical self-care, such as regular exercise, healthy eating, and adequate sleep, can have a significant impact on mental health and energy levels.

- **Creative Expression**: Many neurodivergent teens find relief from masking and stress through creative outlets like drawing, writing, music, or crafts. Encourage your daughter to explore hobbies that allow her to express herself freely.

Real-Life Example:

Hannah, a 16-year-old with ADHD, found that she was able to reduce her anxiety by incorporating self-care practices into her routine.

She started taking short walks after school to decompress, and her parents encouraged her to create art as a way to express her emotions. These practices helped her manage the stress of masking and prevent burnout.

Therapy: A Safe Space to Unmask

Therapy can play an important role in helping neurodivergent teens unmask and address the psychological toll of pretending to be "normal." A therapist trained in working with neurodivergent individuals can help your daughter explore her emotions, understand the roots of her anxiety or depression, and develop coping strategies for reducing the need to mask.

Therapy also provides a safe space where your daughter can express herself without judgment, which is essential for building confidence and emotional resilience. Cognitive Behavioral Therapy (CBT), Dialectical Behavioral Therapy (DBT), and Sensory Integration Therapy are some of the therapies that can help neurodivergent teens manage anxiety, depression, and sensory issues.

Real-Life Example:

After years of masking her true feelings, Sophia, a 15-year-old girl with autism, started therapy with a psychologist who specialized in autism and neurodivergent mental health. Through therapy, Sophia was able to explore her struggles with social interactions and anxiety, learning tools to manage her emotions and reduce the pressure of pretending to be someone she wasn't.

Setting Healthy Boundaries

For neurodivergent teens, setting healthy boundaries is a crucial aspect of self-care. Boundaries protect them from emotional burnout and help them maintain control over their social interactions, schoolwork, and personal time. Teaching your daughter how to communicate her needs, assert her limits, and prioritize her emotional well-being will reduce the strain of constant masking.

Encourage your daughter to:

- **Speak Up About Needs**: Help her understand that it's okay to ask for accommodations or take breaks when she feels overwhelmed.

- **Say "No" When Needed**: Empower her to say no to social events or tasks that feel too overwhelming, teaching her that her emotional health is the priority.

- **Advocate for Herself**: Encourage your daughter to take ownership of her emotional needs and communicate with family, friends, and educators about the support she requires.

Real-Life Example:

Olivia, a 17-year-old girl with ADHD, learned to set boundaries with her friends and teachers. She began speaking up when social situations became overwhelming, politely excusing herself from gatherings or asking for more time to complete assignments. By doing so, Olivia was able to manage her stress levels more effectively and protect her mental health.

Conclusion

Masking is a silent crisis that significantly impacts the mental health and well-being of neurodivergent girls. While masking may allow them to fit into societal expectations, it comes at the cost of emotional and psychological distress, leading to anxiety, depression, burnout, and shutdowns. As parents and caregivers, it is essential to recognize the toll masking takes on our daughters and provide the support, understanding, and tools needed for self-care, therapy, and healthy boundary-setting.

By fostering an environment of empathy, creating opportunities for self-expression, and encouraging self-compassion, we can help our neurodivergent teens navigate their world with confidence and authenticity. With the right support, they can unmask their true selves and thrive emotionally, socially, and academically.

Technology, Screen Time, and Digital Socializing

⎯⎯⎯⎯⎯⎯⎯⎯⎯⎯ ⧓ ⎯⎯⎯⎯⎯⎯⎯⎯⎯⎯

In today's digital age, technology plays a central role in nearly every aspect of life. For neurodivergent girls, technology often serves as both a tool for stimulation and a way to connect socially. The internet provides opportunities for these girls to explore their interests, find supportive communities, and create spaces where they can express themselves freely without the constraints of face-to-face interactions. However, managing screen time and understanding how to use technology in a healthy way are crucial skills, especially when screen time can easily become excessive or replace in-person interactions.

This chapter explores how neurodivergent girls use technology for stimulation and social connection, discusses how to promote healthy screen time habits without shaming digital engagement, and highlights strategies for online safety, involvement in fandoms, and finding meaningful communities in digital spaces.

How Neurodivergent Girls Use Tech for Stimulation and Social Connection

1. The Role of Technology in Stimulation

For many neurodivergent girls, especially those with ADHD or autism, technology offers a way to self-regulate and manage sensory sensitivities. Video games, apps, and even social media can provide a sense of immersion, focus, or comfort that might be difficult to find in other activities. The hyperfocus characteristic of ADHD, for example, often leads these girls to become deeply engaged in video games, YouTube videos, or social media platforms, where they can lose themselves in a world that feels structured and rewarding.

Technology can also be a sensory escape. For example, the visual and auditory stimulation from playing games, watching videos, or listening to music can help distract from sensory overload, offering a temporary break from overwhelming external stimuli. Similarly, certain apps or websites with repetitive tasks or simple interfaces provide calming, predictable experiences that can help ease anxiety or provide structure to a disorganized day.

Real-life example:

Megan, a 13-year-old with ADHD, often finds it hard to concentrate on homework, but she has discovered that playing a particular game on her tablet helps her focus. The game offers a repetitive, soothing rhythm that Megan can lose herself in, which calms her restlessness and helps her return to her studies with renewed focus. For Megan, this kind of tech engagement provides a much-needed sensory outlet.

2. Technology as a Social Connector

Technology also serves as a critical tool for social connection. Neurodivergent girls, particularly those on the autism spectrum, may find in-person social interactions challenging due to difficulties with nonverbal cues, communication, or sensory sensitivities. The anonymity and controlled environment of online spaces offer a way for them to interact with others in a way that feels safer and less overwhelming.

For example, many neurodivergent girls participate in online forums, social media platforms, or multiplayer games where they can connect with like-minded individuals. These platforms provide a space to bond over shared interests and hobbies, such as video games, books, or music, without the pressure of real-time face-to-face interactions. These digital spaces allow them to form relationships based on common interests, bypassing some of the social challenges they face offline.

Real-life example:

Isla, a 15-year-old girl with autism, has always struggled to fit in at school. However, she has found a sense of belonging in an online fandom community centered around her favorite book series. Through discussions and fan art, Isla has developed friendships with other fans who share her passion. These relationships allow her to express herself in ways that are difficult in person, offering a valuable sense of connection and acceptance.

Healthy Habits Without Shaming Screen Time

1. Screen Time and the Balance Between Benefits and Risks

In our digital-first world, it's crucial to acknowledge that **screen time** is not inherently harmful. For neurodivergent girls, technology can be an invaluable tool for learning, socializing, and self-regulation. However, like anything else, balance is key. Prolonged exposure to screens without proper breaks or boundaries can lead to physical and emotional consequences, including eye strain, poor sleep, decreased physical activity, and exacerbated anxiety or depression.

The challenge, therefore, is not in eliminating screen time but in teaching healthy habits that allow technology to complement, rather than replace, other important aspects of life.

Instead of shaming excessive screen time, focus on fostering habits that include breaks, balanced activity, and mindfulness about usage. This includes setting boundaries and limits around the types of technology used, the duration of use, and the time of day screens are used.

2. Setting Healthy Boundaries

Helping neurodivergent girls establish healthy boundaries around screen time involves creating a balance between online engagement and offline activities. This can include:

- **Screen time limits**: Set reasonable time limits for daily technology use to encourage breaks and physical activity. Tools like Apple's Screen Time feature or Android's Digital Wellbeing settings allow for setting app limits and daily use restrictions.

- **Offline activities**: Encourage a variety of activities that don't involve screens, such as reading, cooking, sports, or other creative hobbies. Having a balance of activities can prevent screen time from becoming excessive.

- **Mindful use**: Instead of using technology as a distraction, encourage your daughter to engage with it purposefully. For example, using it to learn new skills, engage in creative projects, or socialize with friends can provide more meaningful experiences compared to mindless scrolling or gaming.

Real-life example:

Charlotte, a 16-year-old with ADHD, loves watching YouTube videos and playing online games. However, her parents noticed that her gaming habit was becoming excessive, leading her to neglect homework and sleep. They introduced a structured routine where Charlotte could enjoy gaming in the evenings but had to take breaks during the day for exercise and other hobbies. Charlotte appreciated having set limits because it allowed her to continue enjoying her favorite activities without sacrificing her health or responsibilities.

3. Encouraging Self-Reflection Around Technology Use

Incorporating self-reflection into screen time habits can also be a valuable tool. Encourage your daughter to monitor how she feels after using technology for extended periods. Does it make her feel energized or drained? Is she using it to cope with stress or anxiety? Helping her become more aware of her digital habits and their emotional impacts can give her the tools to manage technology use independently.

Real-life example:

Olivia, a 14-year-old with autism, often used social media to cope with feelings of loneliness. Over time, she noticed that after scrolling through Instagram or Twitter for hours, she felt more anxious and disconnected. With the help of her parents, Olivia began limiting her social media use to a set time each day and shifted her focus to creative outlets like drawing and writing. She felt more balanced and in control of her emotions.

Online Safety, Fandoms, and Finding Community

1. Online Safety: Protecting Her Digital Space

For neurodivergent girls, the internet can be a double-edged sword. While it offers opportunities for social connection and personal growth, it also exposes them to potential risks, including online predators, cyberbullying, and harmful content. It's essential to teach your daughter about online safety and how to protect her personal information in digital spaces.

Some essential online safety strategies include:

- **Privacy settings**: Encourage your daughter to use strong privacy settings on social media platforms and apps. Limit who can view her posts, message her, or see her personal information.

- **Safe online communication**: Teach your daughter to communicate with trusted individuals and avoid sharing sensitive personal information with strangers. Make sure she knows how to block or report anyone who makes her feel uncomfortable online.

- **Recognizing red flags**: Help her recognize potential risks, such as requests for personal information, strangers trying to meet in real life, or inappropriate content. Empower her to trust her instincts and seek help if something doesn't feel right.

Real-life example:

Maya, a 15-year-old with ADHD, was an active member of several online gaming communities. While she enjoyed the social aspects of these platforms, she wasn't always aware of the potential risks. Her parents helped her set up her privacy settings, showed her how to report inappropriate behavior, and established rules about online interactions. Maya now feels safer in her digital spaces and is more confident in managing her online presence.

2. Fandoms as a Safe Social Outlet

Fandoms—communities centered around shared interests like books, TV shows, movies, or video games can provide a supportive, safe space for neurodivergent girls to find like-minded individuals who share their passions. These communities often offer a sense of belonging and understanding that may be harder to find in school or other offline spaces. In fandoms, neurodivergent girls can express their interests and engage in positive interactions with others who accept them for who they are.

Real-life example:

Emily, a 17-year-old girl with autism, struggled to make friends at school but found solace in a Harry Potter fandom group online. Through discussions, fan fiction, and fan art, Emily was able to form meaningful friendships with people who appreciated her unique perspective. This community provided her with a sense of belonging that she struggled to find in her offline life.

3. Finding Supportive Online Communities

In addition to fandoms, there are numerous online support groups and forums designed specifically for neurodivergent individuals. These spaces provide opportunities to connect with others who understand the challenges and joys of being neurodivergent. Platforms like Reddit, Tumblr, and Discord host communities where neurodivergent girls can share experiences, exchange advice, and form supportive networks.

When seeking out these communities, it's important to prioritize those that are safe, inclusive, and positive. Look for groups that focus on acceptance and empowerment rather than judgment or negativity.

Real-life example:

Hannah, a 16-year-old with ADHD, joined an online community for ADHD support where members shared tips for managing their symptoms and celebrated each other's successes. Through this group, she gained valuable insights into her condition and found the support and understanding that she had been lacking in her real-world interactions.

Conclusion

Technology can be a powerful tool for neurodivergent girls, providing opportunities for learning, social connection, and personal expression. However, as with any tool, it's important to use it mindfully and responsibly. By teaching your daughter how to balance her screen time, prioritize self-care, and navigate online spaces safely, you can help her harness the benefits of technology while avoiding potential risks.

Fandoms and online communities offer spaces for neurodivergent girls to find acceptance, build connections, and explore their passions in a way that feels comfortable and empowering. By guiding her to healthy digital habits, you help ensure that technology becomes a positive force in her life, rather than a source of stress or harm.

In a world that is increasingly digital, it's crucial to acknowledge that technology isn't just a means of entertainment—it's also a vital tool for building community, expressing identity, and finding support. By fostering a healthy relationship with technology, you can help your daughter thrive both online and offline.

CHAPTER 11

Building Self-Esteem in a World That Doesn't Get Her

Neurodivergent girls often grow up feeling misunderstood, whether it's because they don't meet societal expectations of behavior, struggle to navigate social situations, or face challenges that others can't comprehend. These girls may feel like they're constantly too much or not enough: *too sensitive*, *too loud*, *too quiet*, or *too different* from the "norm." This gap between their internal experiences and the world's expectations can lead to feelings of inadequacy and low self-esteem. Yet, with the right guidance and support, neurodivergent girls can learn to embrace their unique qualities, reject negative stereotypes, and cultivate a sense of self-worth. This chapter explores how to build self-esteem in neurodivergent girls by challenging internalized self-doubt and fostering identity-affirming practices that help them recognize their strengths.

Why Neurodivergent Girls Often Feel "Too Much" or "Not Enough"

1. The Struggle Between Internal Experience and External Expectations

Neurodivergent girls often find themselves caught between who they are internally and how the world expects them to behave. Whether it's an anxiety disorder, ADHD, autism, or sensory processing issues, neurodivergent traits can lead to behaviors that are perceived as "disruptive," "awkward," or "overreacting." Society tends to praise qualities like emotional regulation, social fluency, and cognitive flexibility, often overlooking the strengths that neurodivergent girls possess. This mismatch creates a deep sense of confusion and internal conflict—teens feel like they're constantly failing to meet the expectations set by others, leading to feelings of inadequacy.

For example, a neurodivergent girl who has difficulty maintaining eye contact may be seen as uninterested or rude, even though her discomfort with eye contact is simply part of her neurodivergence. Similarly, a girl with ADHD may be labeled as "too talkative" or "too impulsive" when these behaviors stem from challenges with attention regulation, not a lack of desire to engage appropriately.

Real-life example:

Amelia, a 16-year-old girl with autism, constantly feels "too much" in social situations. She is highly sensitive to sensory inputs like bright lights and loud sounds, but when she expresses discomfort, others often brush it off as being overly dramatic. At school, Amelia is often told that she's "too shy" or "too different" when she has trouble making friends or engaging in group activities. This has led to a constant feeling of inadequacy. Amelia believes that no matter how hard she tries, she will always fall short of what others expect from her, making her question her worth.

2. Self-Perception: "Not Enough" and the Fear of Being Different

On the flip side, many neurodivergent girls struggle with feeling "not enough." When they cannot conform to the expectations of others, they begin to internalize the idea that they are somehow lacking or defective. This feeling of "not enough" often stems from messages received from peers, teachers, or even family members who do not understand the challenges neurodivergent girls face. The social expectations placed upon them may lead them to feel like they have to "fit in" or "perform" in ways that don't align with their true self.

This phenomenon is particularly prominent during adolescence, a time when the desire to fit in is strong. When neurodivergent girls experience difficulty conforming to social norms—such as socializing, maintaining friendships, or participating in class—they can feel alienated or disconnected from their peers. They may feel that they are inherently wrong or broken because they don't fit into the mold of what society expects.

Real-life example:

Zara, a 15-year-old girl with ADHD, feels like she's constantly *too much* or *not enough*. She often forgets things, speaks impulsively, and struggles with organization, leading her to be reprimanded at school. While Zara's classmates seem to excel in social situations, she feels she's always *missing* something, and her struggles lead her to think she's not capable of being a "normal" teenager. This self-doubt leads to anxiety and low self-esteem, as Zara begins to believe that no matter how hard she tries, she will never live up to expectations.

3. Gendered Expectations for Neurodivergent Girls

Girls, in particular, face unique pressures when it comes to societal expectations. While boys with neurodivergent traits like ADHD or autism are often recognized and supported early, girls tend to mask their symptoms to avoid being perceived as "too different." Additionally, girls are expected to be more socially intuitive and emotionally regulated, traits that many neurodivergent girls struggle with. As a result, they may feel out of place in social contexts, which can exacerbate feelings of loneliness, shame, and isolation.

The struggle to meet gendered expectations of emotional regulation, social interaction, and appearance can further contribute to feelings of being "too much" or "not enough." These pressures often make neurodivergent girls feel that they are failing to meet the criteria set by society, leading them to internalize negative beliefs about themselves.

Countering Self-Doubt with Identity-Affirming Practices

1. Reframing Self-Talk: Challenging Negative Beliefs

One of the first steps in building self-esteem for neurodivergent girls is challenging the negative self-talk that reinforces feelings of inadequacy. Self-doubt is often fueled by the belief that neurodivergent traits are defects or flaws. Teaching neurodivergent girls to reframe these beliefs can help them shift their perception of themselves.

For example, instead of seeing impulsivity as "a problem," help your daughter view it as a part of her unique brain wiring. Impulsivity may sometimes lead to mistakes, but it can also be linked to creativity, spontaneity, and a willingness to take risks. By emphasizing the strengths and positives that come with neurodivergent traits, girls can learn to view themselves more holistically, embracing their differences rather than seeing them as something to hide or change.

Real-life example:

Lia, a 14-year-old girl with ADHD, often thought of her distractibility as a weakness. However, through therapy, Lia learned to reframe her self-talk. Instead of thinking, "I'm not able to focus," she started to think, "I have a mind that loves to jump between ideas, and that can help me solve problems in creative ways." This new perspective shifted Lia's view of herself, empowering her to see her neurodivergent traits as strengths, not weaknesses.

2. Practicing Self-Compassion: Embracing Imperfection

Neurodivergent girls often hold themselves to unattainably high standards because they have been taught that they need to be "perfect" in order to be accepted. The reality is that everyone has strengths and weaknesses, and imperfection is part of being human. Teaching self-compassion helps neurodivergent girls acknowledge that their neurodivergent traits are not flaws but parts of their individual identity that make them unique.

Encourage your daughter to practice self-compassion by treating herself with kindness when things don't go as planned. This could involve reminding her that setbacks are a normal part of growth and development and that it's okay to make mistakes.

Real-life example:

Sienna, a 16-year-old with autism, often criticized herself when she made mistakes in social situations. After attending therapy focused on self-compassion, she learned to say things like, "It's okay that I didn't understand that social cue. I'll try again next time." By practicing self-compassion, Sienna began to embrace her unique way of interacting with others and developed greater resilience.

3. Celebrating Neurodivergent Strengths

Instead of focusing on perceived deficits, it's important to highlight and celebrate the strengths of neurodivergent girls. For example, many neurodivergent girls excel in creative thinking, problem-solving, attention to detail, and empathy. These strengths should be recognized and nurtured.

Creating a strengths-based environment at home or school, where neurodivergent traits are seen as assets rather than challenges, can help your daughter develop a positive sense of self-worth. Celebrate her accomplishments, even small ones, and encourage her to pursue passions that align with her natural talents and abilities.

Real-life example:

Jasmine, a 17-year-old with ADHD, struggled with academic tasks but excelled in art and design. Her parents supported her by encouraging her to pursue her creative interests, even though they didn't always align with traditional school subjects. By focusing on her creative talents and giving her the freedom to explore her artistic abilities, Jasmine developed a strong sense of pride in her work and a renewed sense of self-worth.

Positive Role Models and Inner Strength

1. Role Models Who Understand

One of the most powerful ways to help neurodivergent girls build self-esteem is by introducing them to positive role models—individuals who share similar neurodivergent traits and have succeeded in overcoming challenges. These role models provide a living example that it is possible to thrive while embracing neurodivergence.

Role models could include public figures with ADHD, autism, or other neurodivergent traits, such as actors, musicians, writers, or scientists who have openly discussed their struggles and successes. It can also include local mentors, teachers, or community members who serve as everyday examples of strength and perseverance.

Real-life example:

Abigail, a 15-year-old girl with ADHD, was inspired by a well-known YouTuber who openly discussed her ADHD and the challenges she faced growing up. Seeing how this role model used her unique traits to create a successful career helped Abigail understand that she, too, could find success while embracing her neurodivergent qualities.

2. Building Inner Strength: Mindfulness and Resilience

Encouraging your daughter to build inner strength through practices like mindfulness, meditation, or journaling can help her manage stress and build resilience. These practices encourage self-reflection and help neurodivergent girls develop emotional regulation skills that increase their confidence in handling challenges.

Real-life example:

Maya, a 16-year-old girl with autism, started practicing mindfulness to help manage her anxiety. She used breathing exercises and journaling to process her feelings and develop strategies for dealing with overwhelming situations. Over time, Maya felt more in control of her emotions and more confident in handling the challenges that came her way.

Conclusion

Building self-esteem in neurodivergent girls requires patience, empathy, and a strong commitment to helping them embrace their unique identities. By countering self-doubt with identity-affirming practices, encouraging self-compassion, and providing positive role models, we can empower neurodivergent girls to see their differences as strengths rather than weaknesses. Supporting them in celebrating their neurodivergent traits—whether through creative outlets, personal accomplishments, or simply accepting imperfections—helps cultivate a resilient sense of self-worth that will serve them throughout their lives. With the right guidance, neurodivergent girls can learn to navigate a world that doesn't always "get" them with confidence, pride, and authenticity.

CHAPTER 12

Scripting Independence Teaching Life Skills with Compassion

———————— ⬨✕⬨ ————————

A s neurodivergent girls grow older, one of the most important goals for both parents and educators is fostering independence. However, teaching life skills to neurodivergent girls can be a complex task due to challenges with executive function, emotional regulation, and anxiety. Executive function skills such as planning, organizing, managing time, and self-regulating are essential for performing daily responsibilities, but these skills don't always come naturally to neurodivergent individuals. This chapter explores how to teach life skills with compassion by breaking down executive function skills, turning everyday routines into meaningful rituals, and helping neurodivergent girls build autonomy while minimizing anxiety.

Executive Function Meets Real-World Responsibilities

1. The Link Between Executive Function and Independence

At the core of independence is executive function, a collection of cognitive processes that enable individuals to manage tasks and responsibilities. These include skills like:

- **Planning and organization**: The ability to map out and execute tasks in a systematic way.

- **Time management**: The ability to allocate appropriate amounts of time for tasks and avoid procrastination.

- **Self-monitoring**: The ability to track progress and adjust actions as needed.

- **Emotional regulation**: Managing emotional responses to challenges, stress, or frustration.

- **Impulse control**: The ability to resist distractions and stay focused on tasks.

For neurodivergent girls, these executive function skills can be harder to develop. ADHD, autism, or other neurodivergent conditions often result in difficulties with organization, time management, and emotional regulation, which in turn can lead to struggles with real-world responsibilities. Household chores, managing schoolwork, and organizing personal belongings can feel overwhelming or unmanageable.

Real-life example:

Maya, a 14-year-old girl with ADHD, often struggles with completing tasks like making her bed, doing homework, and keeping her room tidy. She starts many tasks with enthusiasm but frequently gets sidetracked, leaving her with incomplete projects and a sense of failure. Maya's challenges stem from executive function difficulties, which makes it harder for her to prioritize tasks and manage her time effectively.

2. Breaking Tasks Down Into Manageable Steps

One of the most effective strategies for teaching life skills to neurodivergent girls is to break tasks down into smaller, more manageable steps. Instead of overwhelming your daughter with a large, abstract goal, focus on the individual components of the task. For instance, making the bed can be broken down into:

1. Straightening the sheets.

2. Fluffing the pillows.

3. Pulling the blanket into place.

By simplifying tasks, neurodivergent girls can approach them with more clarity and less frustration. Moreover, breaking tasks into steps gives them a concrete way to measure their progress, boosting their confidence and sense of accomplishment.

Real-life example:

When Samira, a 15-year-old girl with autism, was asked to clean her room, the task felt too overwhelming for her. Her parents began by breaking the task into smaller steps, such as "put clothes in the hamper," "organize the bookshelf," and "sweep the floor." Samira was able to manage these smaller tasks more easily, and with each completed step, she gained a sense of success and independence.

Turning Routines into Rituals, Not Chores

1. The Power of Meaningful Routines

For neurodivergent girls, turning everyday routines into rituals can significantly improve their relationship with daily responsibilities. While the concept of "chores" can feel burdensome or overwhelming, rituals are imbued with a sense of purpose and personal meaning. By transforming repetitive tasks into rituals, you can make these activities more engaging, enjoyable, and fulfilling.

A ritual doesn't just involve completing a task; it's about embedding personal significance and mindfulness into that activity. This is particularly important for neurodivergent girls who may have sensory sensitivities or emotional dysregulation, as the act of incorporating mindfulness can make a task feel more soothing and structured.

For instance, instead of simply "doing laundry," you can create a ritual around the process. Perhaps it involves choosing a favorite scented detergent, using a specific routine to fold clothes, or incorporating music or a favorite podcast into the experience.

Real-life example:

Olivia, a 16-year-old with ADHD, had difficulty completing her homework assignments because they felt like a burden. Her parents decided to make homework time a ritual by allowing Olivia to choose a special snack, setting up a cozy workspace with her favorite playlist, and creating a checklist to track her progress. Olivia found that by turning homework into a personalized ritual, it became easier to focus and more enjoyable. Over time, this approach not only improved her academic performance but also helped her manage time more effectively.

2. Mindfulness in Routine Tasks

Introducing mindfulness into routine activities—whether it's brushing teeth, making the bed, or preparing meals helps neurodivergent girls engage in the moment and develop a sense of self-awareness. Mindfulness allows them to become more present, reducing anxiety and preventing their minds from getting overwhelmed by the complexity of the task.

For example, when your daughter is cleaning her room, encourage her to focus on the feeling of the broom against the floor or the scent of the cleaning spray. These small sensory experiences can make the activity feel more grounded and enjoyable.

Real-life example:

Zoe, a 17-year-old girl with autism, struggled with sensory sensitivities that made everyday tasks feel overwhelming. Her parents encouraged her to focus on the textures and sounds of the tasks like the softness of a towel or the rhythm of vacuuming rather than the task itself. This allowed Zoe to approach daily chores with less anxiety and more mindfulness.

Helping Her Build Autonomy Without Anxiety

1. Supporting Independence Through Structure

One of the primary goals for neurodivergent girls is to build autonomy allowing them to take responsibility for their actions, choices, and tasks. However, for many, this goal can feel intimidating, especially if they've struggled with executive function challenges in the past. The key is to provide structure without overwhelming them.

Structured independence involves creating routines and systems that provide a sense of stability while still allowing for personal choice. This might mean setting consistent times for specific activities (like doing homework after school or cleaning the room on weekends) but giving your daughter control over how she completes the task. For example, she might have the choice of which cleaning supplies to use or which order to complete chores in, but the overall structure remains intact.

Real-life example:

Maria, a 15-year-old with ADHD, struggled with managing her homework assignments. Her parents helped her create a consistent routine where she would spend 30 minutes on schoolwork each afternoon after coming home from school. Within this structure, Maria was given the autonomy to decide which subject to start with and how to break down her tasks. This combination of structure and autonomy gave her the confidence to tackle her responsibilities without feeling overwhelmed.

2. Reducing Anxiety Through Positive Reinforcement

Building autonomy in a way that doesn't provoke anxiety requires a careful balance. Positive reinforcement, rewarding efforts rather than focusing solely on outcomes can help your daughter feel confident and motivated without the pressure of perfection.

Recognize small victories and provide praise for effort and perseverance, not just completion. This helps neurodivergent girls see that progress, not perfection, is the goal. Additionally, reinforcing positive habits encourages them to build self-confidence and internal motivation.

Real-life example:

Hannah, a 16-year-old with autism, found it difficult to stick with new routines, especially when she was unsure of the results. Her parents made sure to praise her when she followed through with her daily responsibilities, whether it was completing a task independently or simply starting the task on time. By focusing on effort and persistence, Hannah learned to value the process of building independence, which in turn helped her reduce anxiety around new tasks.

3. Gradual Release of Responsibility

Building autonomy is a gradual process that requires a release of responsibility. Parents and caregivers should avoid micromanaging every task or stepping in too quickly when something goes wrong. Instead, provide scaffolding and gradually reduce the level of support as your daughter gains confidence and skill.

For example, if your daughter is learning to cook, you might start by guiding her through the steps. As she becomes more competent, you can reduce the amount of direction you provide, allowing her to handle more of the task independently.

Real-life example:

Lily, a 14-year-old with ADHD, wanted to learn how to cook. Her parents initially helped her by preparing the ingredients and guiding her through each step. Over time, Lily was given more independence in the kitchen, starting with small tasks like chopping vegetables. Eventually, she was able to make full meals on her own, feeling a sense of pride in her growing skills.

Conclusion

Teaching neurodivergent girls life skills especially those that foster independence is a delicate and empowering process. By focusing on executive function skills, turning daily routines into meaningful rituals, and helping them build autonomy without anxiety, we provide the structure, support, and confidence they need to succeed. Neurodivergent girls are capable of becoming independent and self-sufficient, but they need the tools, space, and encouragement to develop these crucial skills at their own pace. By focusing on their strengths, allowing for gradual development, and offering compassionate support, we can help them thrive as they learn to navigate the world with confidence, resilience, and self-reliance.

CHAPTER 13

Talking About the Future College, Work, and Adulting

———⟨⟩✕⟨⟩———

The future can be an overwhelming concept, especially when it is framed through the lens of societal expectations and conventional definitions of success. For neurodivergent individuals, particularly those with ADHD or autism, the traditional markers of success like college graduation, securing a job, or achieving a certain social standing may not resonate in the same way they do for neurotypical peers. The traditional path to adulthood can be an intimidating and even discouraging concept for neurodivergent individuals, who may feel that the conventional milestones don't fit their strengths, needs, or desires.

In this chapter, we'll explore how neurodivergent individuals, particularly teens with ADHD or autism, can reframe their understanding of success. We will also discuss how to create an individualized transition plan that helps them move through the stages of life, college, work, and adult responsibilities on their terms. Finally, we'll consider the importance of encouraging teens to dream in their own language, allowing them to envision a future that reflects their authentic selves rather than a cookie-cutter vision of success.

Rethinking Success: Neurodivergent Definitions of Fulfillment

Success, as traditionally defined, often revolves around a set of socially agreed-upon milestones: obtaining a college degree, finding a stable job, owning a home, and achieving a certain social status. These goals are often presented as essential benchmarks of adult life. However, for many neurodivergent individuals, especially those with ADHD and autism, the traditional path to success may not align with their strengths, interests, or ways of engaging with the world.

The Conventional Model of Success and Its Limitations

The conventional model of success often centers around certain ideals that can feel exclusionary to those who think and operate differently. This might include:

- **Academic Achievement**: Graduation from high school, obtaining a college degree, and excelling academically are traditional markers of success. However, many neurodivergent individuals struggle with the structure and demands of formal education. For instance, someone with ADHD might find the rigid structure of a classroom, long hours of study, and expectation for sustained attention to be a source of stress and frustration.

- **Work and Career**: For many, a stable, nine-to-five job is the ideal of professional success. The standard workplace often assumes a one-size-fits-all approach, valuing traits like punctuality, social norms, and consistent productivity. For someone on the autism spectrum, these same traits can be an exhausting struggle. Similarly, for someone with ADHD, staying focused in a traditional office setting may be incredibly challenging.

- **Social Conformity**: Much of the traditional concept of success involves fitting into social structures—marriage, family life, and community roles. Social pressures can feel overwhelming for those who find social interactions difficult or draining.

While the traditional markers of success are valid for some, they do not account for the diverse ways that neurodivergent individuals experience fulfillment. For many people with ADHD or autism, fulfillment does not necessarily come from fitting into the established mold but from creating a life that aligns with their unique way of being.

Neurodivergent Definitions of Fulfillment

Instead of following the traditional markers of success, neurodivergent individuals often find fulfillment in ways that are more personalized and reflective of their specific strengths and values. Success, for them, might be measured by personal growth, the ability to pursue passions, and the development of a lifestyle that supports their well-being.

For ADHD individuals, fulfillment might come from:

- **Creative Expression**: Many individuals with ADHD excel in creative pursuits that allow for flexibility and spontaneous thinking. Careers in art, music, design, or writing may be more fulfilling for someone with ADHD who needs to channel their energetic and often unconventional ideas in productive ways.

- **Entrepreneurship**: The typical workplace structure may not always appeal to individuals with ADHD. Entrepreneurship, where there is more flexibility and autonomy, might be a more satisfying path. ADHD individuals often thrive when they have the freedom to direct their own projects and set their own schedules.

- **Dynamic Work Environments**: Jobs that offer variety and excitement, such as those in the media, sales, or event management, can be particularly fulfilling. The ability to switch tasks and work in a dynamic, fast-paced environment suits the ADHD brain, which thrives in conditions that allow for constant stimulation and flexibility.

For autistic individuals, fulfillment might come from:

- **Specialized Interests**: Many individuals on the autism spectrum develop deep expertise in a particular area. Fulfillment may come from pursuing careers that allow them to engage deeply with their interests, such as science, technology, history, or art. For example, an autistic individual with a passion for coding may find fulfillment in a career as a software developer.

- **Structured Environments**: Unlike the chaotic and unstructured environments that can overwhelm some people with ADHD, many individuals with autism prefer clear, predictable routines and structured environments. A career in fields like research, library science, or data analysis might align with their strengths, providing a sense of accomplishment and satisfaction from systematic work.

- **Independent Work**: Many individuals with autism prefer working independently or in quiet, low-stimulation settings. Remote work, freelance opportunities, or careers that allow for solitary work can provide the peace and focus necessary for autistic individuals to thrive.

Rethinking success for neurodivergent individuals involves validating their individual needs, strengths, and passions. It means recognizing that success is not a one-size-fits-all concept and that fulfillment is often best found when individuals are able to embrace their authentic selves.

Transition Planning for Teens with ADHD or Autism

For teens with ADHD or autism, the transition from high school to adulthood can feel particularly daunting. The traditional educational system, which often assumes a uniform developmental trajectory, may not provide the structure and support that neurodivergent students need. Transition planning, which helps prepare teens for the next stages of their lives, whether that means entering the workforce, attending college, or pursuing other avenues, requires a personalized approach that takes their unique needs into account.

1. Creating a Personalized Transition Plan

A personalized transition plan is a roadmap that helps teens with ADHD or autism navigate the steps required for a successful transition to adulthood. This plan should be flexible, recognizing the individual's specific needs, goals, and preferences. A well-crafted transition plan takes into account factors such as:

- **Academic and Career Goals**: Understanding what types of work or education align with the individual's strengths is crucial. This might include identifying potential career interests, exploring college options, or considering apprenticeships or vocational training.

- **Life Skills Development**: Transition planning should include practical life skills, such as money management, time management, self-advocacy, and independent living skills. These skills are vital for navigating adult responsibilities and ensuring that the teen has the tools needed to succeed in the world outside of school.

- **Support Systems**: Ensuring that the teen has a network of support, whether it's family, mentors, or support groups—is key to successful transitioning. Teens with ADHD or autism may benefit from accommodations in higher education or the workplace, so having a plan for accessing these resources is important.

2. Exploring College and Career Options

When it comes to college, neurodivergent teens may face additional hurdles that require careful consideration and planning. While college may be a great fit for some neurodivergent individuals, others may find that vocational training, trade schools, or entering the workforce directly are better options.

For ADHD teens, a college environment that offers flexibility in learning formats—such as online courses, project-based learning, or hands on programs—might be more supportive. ADHD students may thrive in environments that allow for self-directed learning and provide options for shorter, more engaging assignments rather than long, lecture-based courses.

For autistic teens, colleges that offer specialized programs or autism-friendly accommodations can be ideal. Some universities provide neurodiversity support offices that help students with autism navigate campus life, access tutoring, and manage social interactions. Additionally, community colleges or smaller institutions may provide a more structured and manageable environment for individuals who may feel overwhelmed by larger campuses.

It's essential to encourage teens to explore a variety of options and to support them in finding a path that aligns with their unique strengths, even if that path does not conform to the traditional "college route."

3. Building Social Skills and Emotional Intelligence

The transition to adulthood also involves navigating social situations and building emotional intelligence. For neurodivergent teens, social interactions can be challenging, and they may need explicit instruction and practice in developing social skills. This might include learning how to engage in conversations, manage conflicts, and build relationships in professional or educational settings.

Emotional intelligence; the ability to recognize, understand, and manage one's emotions is a vital skill for adulthood. This includes developing self-awareness, practicing self-regulation, and learning how to handle stress. Emotional intelligence helps neurodivergent teens handle the uncertainty and challenges that come with transitioning into adulthood, and it empowers them to make informed decisions about their future.

Encouraging Her to Dream in Her Own Language

A critical aspect of helping neurodivergent teens prepare for the future is encouraging them to dream in their own language. The world often expects teens to conform to a specific narrative of success, but neurodivergent individuals have their own unique ways of thinking and experiencing the world. Encouraging them to dream in their own language means supporting them in envisioning a future that feels authentic, fulfilling, and in line with their personal values and strengths.

1. Fostering Autonomy in Goal-Setting

Rather than imposing external definitions of success, encourage neurodivergent teens to set their own goals. This might include discussing their passions, interests, and long-term aspirations. For some teens, these goals might be related to creative or artistic pursuits; for others, they might be focused on technical, scientific, or intellectual endeavors. By helping teens articulate their goals in their own terms, you empower them to create a future that reflects their authentic self.

For example, a teen with ADHD who is interested in technology might dream of becoming a game designer or an app developer. Instead of suggesting a more traditional career path, such as working in a corporate office, help them explore ways to break into the tech industry through internships, online courses, or personal projects. This allows the teen to pursue their passion without feeling pressured to conform to traditional expectations.

2. Encouraging Exploration and Flexibility

Encouraging teens to dream in their own language also involves fostering a mindset of exploration. Neurodivergent individuals often benefit from trying out different experiences and pathways before committing to a specific direction. This can include taking on internships, volunteer positions, or part-time jobs in various fields. By gaining exposure to different environments, neurodivergent teens can better understand what resonates with them and where their strengths lie.

Flexibility is key: while goals are important, it's equally important to recognize that life is full of twists and turns. A neurodivergent teen's path may not be linear, and that's okay. It's important to support them in navigating their journey without forcing them to conform to a rigid timeline or path.

Conclusion

Talking about the future, whether it's college, work, or adulting, can be a daunting task for neurodivergent teens. However, by rethinking success, creating personalized transition plans, and encouraging them to dream in their own language, we can help neurodivergent individuals envision a future that reflects their unique strengths, needs, and desires. By offering the right support, fostering autonomy, and allowing room for flexibility, we can ensure that neurodivergent teens are empowered to move through life's transitions with confidence, resilience, and authenticity.

Supporting Yourself So You Can Support Her

Supporting a neurodivergent daughter is a journey that requires patience, understanding, and resilience. As a parent, caregiver, or guardian, it's easy to become consumed by the needs of your child, often at the expense of your own well-being. The challenges of managing her needs, navigating the complexities of neurodivergence, and advocating for her in a world that may not fully understand can leave you feeling drained, overwhelmed, and self-doubting. However, in order to be the best support for your daughter, it's crucial to take care of yourself first.

This chapter focuses on the importance of self-care and self-compassion for parents and caregivers of neurodivergent girls. It explores how to manage expectations, deal with exhaustion and self-doubt, build a solid support network, and celebrate the small wins, both for your daughter and for yourself. By taking proactive steps to care for your own mental and emotional health, you can be better equipped to help your daughter thrive.

Managing Your Expectations, Exhaustion, and Self-Doubt

1. Understanding and Managing Expectations

As a parent of a neurodivergent child, your expectations may be shaped by societal norms, personal hopes, or pressures from well-meaning family members or friends. It's important to acknowledge that society's standard expectations for neurodivergent children, especially girls, can be both unrealistic and unfair. Many neurodivergent girls experience the world in ways that differ from their peers, which can make it difficult for them to meet traditional academic, social, and behavioral expectations.

As a caregiver, it's essential to redefine your expectations to align with your daughter's unique strengths and challenges. Setting goals based on her individual needs and capabilities, rather than trying to conform to traditional norms, can help you create a more realistic and compassionate approach to her growth and development. Instead of focusing on "what she should be able to do," consider the progress she's made, the small milestones she's achieved, and how you can support her as she develops at her own pace.

Real-life example:

Rachel, a mother of a 14-year-old girl with autism, initially felt frustrated that her daughter, Leah, was not making the same social connections as her peers. She often compared Leah to other kids in their social circle and felt disheartened when Leah didn't meet those social milestones. Over time, Rachel learned to adjust her expectations. Instead of pressuring Leah to fit in with her peers, she celebrated the connections Leah had made in a small, close-knit group of friends who accepted her for who she was. This shift allowed Rachel to focus on Leah's individual growth, rather than trying to fit her into a standard mold.

2. Coping with Exhaustion: Emotional and Physical Fatigue

Supporting a neurodivergent child can be physically and emotionally exhausting. The emotional labor involved in constantly advocating for your child, managing her needs, and navigating educational, social, and medical systems can lead to burnout. The constant vigilance required to ensure that your daughter has the support and accommodations she needs can leave you feeling drained and overwhelmed.

It's important to acknowledge that exhaustion is normal, but it's also essential to take breaks and make time for rest. Regularly checking in with your emotional and physical well-being allows you to identify when you're approaching burnout and gives you the opportunity to take proactive steps toward self-care.

Real-life example:

Samantha, a single mother of a 16-year-old with ADHD, found herself exhausted from balancing her full-time job, caregiving responsibilities, and constant advocacy for her daughter at school. After attending a support group for parents of neurodivergent children, Samantha realized that she had been neglecting her own needs for years. With the support of the group, Samantha began scheduling regular "self-care days," where she would take time to relax, recharge, and engage in activities that brought her joy. This practice of setting boundaries for her own well-being helped her regain her energy and manage her responsibilities with more patience and clarity.

3. Battling Self-Doubt: The Guilt of Feeling Inadequate

As a caregiver, you may sometimes feel inadequate or question your ability to support your daughter effectively. These feelings of self-doubt are not uncommon, especially when you encounter challenges or when things don't seem to be progressing as quickly as you had hoped. It's easy to fall into the trap of thinking that you should be doing more or doing things differently, but it's important to remind yourself that you are doing the best you can.

Guilt is a natural emotion for parents who want to provide the best for their children, but it's crucial not to let it undermine your confidence or self-worth. Instead of focusing on what you might not have done, focus on the progress you and your daughter have made and the love and support you provide. Self-compassion is key in dealing with these feelings.

Real-life example:

Karen, a mother of a 13-year-old girl with sensory processing issues, frequently felt guilty for not being able to provide a "typical" childhood for her daughter. When Karen's daughter struggled with school events, parties, or activities that involved sensory overload, Karen would blame herself for not protecting her daughter from those experiences. However, with guidance from a therapist, Karen began to shift her mindset. She learned to focus on what she could control, such as creating a calm environment at home and working with teachers to implement accommodations. By accepting her limitations and focusing on what she was doing right, Karen was able to release her guilt and continue supporting her daughter with confidence.

Building Your Own Support Network

1. The Importance of a Strong Support System

No parent should have to navigate the challenges of supporting a neurodivergent child alone. Building a support network is essential for your emotional well-being and for gaining the tools and advice you need. This network might include family members, friends, therapists, support groups, or online communities where other parents share similar experiences. Having a reliable support system provides both emotional comfort and practical advice during difficult times.

Real-life example:

Tom and Lisa, parents of a 15-year-old girl with ADHD, found that they were struggling to manage their daughter's school performance and behavioral issues on their own. After joining a local ADHD support group for parents, they connected with other families who shared similar struggles. These parents offered practical strategies for managing homework, routines, and behavior, and they also provided emotional support when Tom and Lisa were feeling overwhelmed. This network not only gave them new tools to support their daughter but also helped them feel less isolated in their journey.

2. Seeking Professional Guidance

While a supportive community is invaluable, it's also important to have access to professional guidance. Therapists, counselors, educational consultants, and specialists can provide expert advice tailored to your daughter's needs. Regular therapy sessions or coaching for both you and your daughter can help you navigate the challenges of neurodivergence in a healthy and constructive way.

Real-life example:

Jennifer, a mother of a 17-year-old with autism, worked with a family therapist who specialized in neurodivergence. The therapist helped Jennifer navigate her daughter's transition into high school and adulthood by developing coping strategies for both her daughter and herself. Through family therapy, Jennifer learned techniques for managing stress, setting boundaries, and practicing self-care. This professional support gave Jennifer the confidence to advocate for her daughter while also taking care of her own mental health.

3. Finding Supportive Online Communities

In today's digital world, online communities can provide a wealth of knowledge, support, and camaraderie for parents of neurodivergent children. Whether it's through Facebook groups, online forums, or parenting blogs, the internet offers a space where you can connect with others who understand your experience. These communities often offer tips, resources, and stories that can help you feel less isolated and more empowered.

Real-life example:

Sarah, a 16-year-old girl with ADHD, has a mother named Rebecca who felt overwhelmed when Sarah was diagnosed. Rebecca turned to a popular online forum for parents of neurodivergent children, where she could share her concerns, ask questions, and receive support from other parents who were going through similar experiences. Through these online interactions, Rebecca was able to gain perspective, learn new coping strategies, and feel more supported in her role as a caregiver.

Celebrating Small Wins—For Her and For You

1. Acknowledging Your Daughter's Progress

Celebrating small wins is an important part of the process of supporting a neurodivergent child. Every step forward, no matter how small, is an accomplishment. Recognizing and celebrating these victories, whether it's a successful school project, improved self-regulation, or progress in therapy, helps reinforce your daughter's sense of self-worth and achievement.

Equally important is celebrating your own wins. As a parent, you are making a difference in your daughter's life every day. Celebrating the small victories in your journey helps keep you motivated and reminds you that progress is being made, even when it feels slow.

Real-life example:

Linda, the mother of a 14-year-old girl with ADHD, began celebrating every small victory, such as her daughter completing her homework on time or remembering to bring her lunch to school. These moments were a big deal for Linda and her daughter, and they celebrated together with small rewards like a special outing or a favorite meal. This not only boosted her daughter's confidence but also helped Linda recognize the value in small, positive changes.

2. Focusing on Progress, Not Perfection

It's easy to get caught up in the idea of perfection, but it's important to focus on progress, not perfection. Both you and your daughter will face setbacks along the way. It's essential to embrace the idea that growth and change are ongoing processes, and that the goal is improvement, not flawlessness. By focusing on progress, you create a mindset that values effort and resilience, rather than unattainable ideals of perfection.

Real-life example:

Amanda, the mother of an 18-year-old with autism, had always hoped her daughter would make friends and excel socially, but this was a difficult area for her. When her daughter managed to have a meaningful conversation with a classmate at lunch, Amanda celebrated that moment as a significant achievement. It wasn't perfection, but it was a step in the right direction. By focusing on progress, Amanda learned to appreciate the journey and the unique milestones her daughter reached.

Conclusion

Supporting a neurodivergent child is both an incredibly rewarding and challenging journey. As a parent or caregiver, it's crucial to take care of your own emotional and physical well-being in order to provide the best support for your daughter. By managing your expectations, seeking support from others, and celebrating the small wins, both for her and for yourself, you can navigate the challenges with resilience and compassion.

Building a strong support network, focusing on progress rather than perfection, and practicing self-compassion will help you remain emotionally and physically resilient as you continue to support your neurodivergent daughter. By nurturing your own well-being, you empower both yourself and your daughter to thrive.

CHAPTER 15

Raising the Volume Advocacy, Voice, and Raising Awareness

———❦⚜❦———

For neurodivergent girls, the journey toward self-empowerment often involves learning how to own their story, advocate for themselves, and raise awareness about their unique needs and strengths. In a world that is often not designed with their experiences in mind, having a strong voice is a powerful tool that can help them navigate educational, social, and professional environments. However, for many neurodivergent girls, the idea of speaking up for themselves can feel intimidating or even shameful. It's essential for parents, caregivers, and educators to foster a culture of self-advocacy and awareness, allowing neurodivergent girls to reclaim their narrative and live their lives unapologetically.

This chapter delves into how to help neurodivergent girls own their story without shame, why advocacy is an essential life skill, and how to transition from a "checklist" mentality to embracing a more fluid and personalized roadmap to success. By empowering neurodivergent girls to advocate for themselves, we equip them with the tools they need to confidently navigate their world and raise awareness about neurodivergence for others.

How to Help Her Own Her Story Without Shame

1. The Power of Owning One's Story

Every neurodivergent girl has a unique story to tell. However, societal stigma and a lack of understanding can make it difficult for them to share their experiences openly. Many neurodivergent girls internalize feelings of shame, thinking that their differences are something to hide or be ashamed of. In truth, neurodivergence is not a flaw or a weakness—it is a part of who they are. Helping them embrace their neurodivergent identity without shame is a critical step toward empowerment.

Owning her story means that she accepts and celebrates her neurodivergence, recognizing that it shapes her perspective, strengths, and abilities. When neurodivergent girls are encouraged to share their experiences without fear of judgment, they feel validated and supported, which in turn boosts their confidence and self-esteem.

Real-life example:

Emily, a 16-year-old girl with autism, struggled with explaining her social challenges to her classmates. She often felt embarrassed about her tendency to avoid eye contact or her difficulty with group interactions. With the support of her parents, Emily began to write in a journal about her experiences, acknowledging both her challenges and strengths. Over time, Emily became more comfortable sharing her story with her peers, and she even participated in a school presentation about neurodiversity. By owning her story, Emily felt empowered to advocate for herself and educate others about her needs.

2. Reframing Neurodivergence: From Shame to Strength

To help a neurodivergent girl own her story, it's essential to shift the narrative around neurodivergence from one of shame to strength. Instead of focusing on what is "wrong" with neurodivergence, celebrate what is right, the unique ways in which her brain works, the skills she possesses, and the contributions she can make to the world. This reframing allows neurodivergent girls to see themselves as capable individuals with a valuable perspective to offer.

A great way to start this process is by involving her in conversations about neurodiversity and helping her understand that her experiences are valid. This can be done through books, podcasts, or online communities that center on neurodivergent voices. Encourage her to engage with others who share similar experiences, fostering a sense of belonging and community.

Real-life example:

Sarah, a 17-year-old with ADHD, often felt misunderstood because of her impulsivity and tendency to interrupt others. Her teachers and peers saw these behaviors as disruptive. However, when her mother introduced Sarah to a podcast hosted by neurodivergent individuals, Sarah began to understand that her brain worked differently—not worse, just differently. She learned to see her impulsivity as part of her creativity and energy, rather than as a flaw. This shift in perspective allowed Sarah to embrace her ADHD as a source of strength rather than shame.

Advocacy as a Life Skill

1. The Importance of Self-Advocacy

Self-advocacy is one of the most powerful life skills a neurodivergent girl can develop. Advocating for herself—whether it's requesting accommodations at school, asking for support at work, or simply expressing her needs to friends and family—helps her build confidence and independence. Teaching her how to articulate her needs, recognize her rights, and assert herself in a way that respects both her and others is key to living a fulfilling life.

Advocacy goes beyond just asking for accommodations—it's about asserting her worth, recognizing her strengths, and understanding that her voice is valuable in every context. Whether it's navigating the educational system or preparing for a job interview, self-advocacy enables neurodivergent girls to navigate the world with autonomy and self-assurance.

Real-life example:

Lilly, an 18-year-old with autism, was preparing to go to college and felt anxious about how she would manage social interactions and classroom expectations. Her parents worked with her to develop a self-advocacy plan, where Lilly identified specific accommodations she might need, such as a quiet space during exams and extra time to process information. During her first semester, Lilly confidently approached her professors to discuss her needs, ensuring that she received the support she required to succeed. By advocating for herself, Lilly took control of her educational experience and felt empowered to navigate college life.

2. Teaching Advocacy Skills: Starting Early

Advocacy is a skill that can be taught from a young age, and it's essential to start early in order to build confidence and competence. For neurodivergent girls, this might involve practicing how to ask for help, teaching them to communicate their sensory needs, or discussing ways to express discomfort in social situations. By teaching advocacy skills early on, parents and caregivers can help neurodivergent girls feel empowered to manage their environment and their relationships effectively.

One of the most important aspects of self-advocacy is teaching girls how to recognize when something isn't working and how to ask for changes. Whether it's at school, work, or in social settings, teaching your daughter that it's okay to ask for what she needs sets the foundation for a lifetime of confident self-advocacy.

Real-life example:

Maya, a 15-year-old girl with ADHD, often struggled to focus in large classrooms due to noise distractions. Her mother began practicing advocacy skills with her, role-playing how Maya could ask her teachers for seating arrangements that would minimize distractions. Over time, Maya became more comfortable advocating for herself, not only in the classroom but also in extracurricular activities. This skill helped her feel more in control of her learning environment and empowered her to manage her education on her terms.

Leaving the Checklist Behind—Embracing a Roadmap

1. The Limiting Nature of Checklists

For neurodivergent girls, a strict, one-size-fits-all approach to life—such as following checklists or adhering to rigid milestones—can feel stifling and overwhelming. While checklists can be useful tools for managing tasks, they do not capture the fluidity and uniqueness of each individual's journey. Neurodivergent girls often experience the world differently, which means their paths to success, fulfillment, and happiness may look vastly different from the societal norm.

Instead of focusing on checklists that prioritize external markers of success—such as graduation, employment, or independence—consider embracing a more personalized roadmap that focuses on your daughter's goals, strengths, and values. A roadmap allows for flexibility and adaptability, acknowledging that success doesn't have to follow a linear trajectory.

Real-life example:

Nina, a 19-year-old with ADHD, had always felt burdened by the checklist approach to success. From an early age, she was told that she had to follow a clear path: graduate from high school, go to college, get a job, and eventually get married. However, Nina's true passions lay in pursuing a career as a freelance writer and traveling the world. By embracing a more flexible roadmap for her future, Nina was able to take ownership of her journey. She worked as a freelance writer, traveled extensively, and found success on her own terms, proving that a roadmap can be as unique as the individual walking it.

2. Creating a Personal Roadmap for the Future

A roadmap is an individualized plan that reflects your daughter's unique strengths, needs, and interests. It's not about achieving external goals but about navigating the journey in a way that aligns with her authentic self. Creating a personalized roadmap involves:

- **Identifying her passions and interests**: Encourage your daughter to explore different fields, hobbies, or career paths that resonate with her strengths and values.

- **Setting realistic, flexible goals**: Instead of adhering to rigid milestones, set goals that are adaptable to her evolving interests and needs.

- **Focusing on self-discovery**: The roadmap should prioritize **self-exploration**, allowing your daughter the freedom to discover who she is and what she truly wants out of life.

- **Embracing setbacks and growth**: A roadmap recognizes that setbacks are a part of life. It's not about being perfect, but about growing, learning, and adapting along the way.

Real-life example:

Rachel, a 20-year-old with autism, had been told all her life that success meant attending college and getting a corporate job. However, Rachel found fulfillment in graphic design and social media marketing. With the support of her family, she created a roadmap that involved online design courses, freelance projects, and networking with like-minded individuals. Instead of following a rigid checklist, Rachel focused on creating a career that allowed her to work from home and express her creativity. This personalized approach empowered Rachel to embrace her passions and live a life true to herself.

Conclusion

Raising neurodivergent girls requires helping them find their voice and advocate for themselves in a world that doesn't always understand or accommodate their needs. By teaching them to own their story without shame, empowering them with self-advocacy skills, and helping them move beyond the traditional checklist toward a more personalized roadmap, we can provide them with the tools to navigate their future with confidence.

The road to self-empowerment is not linear, but with the right support, neurodivergent girls can create their own definitions of success, pursue fulfilling careers, and live lives that honor their unique strengths and passions. It is essential for parents and caregivers to support this journey by embracing flexibility, fostering self-compassion, and encouraging their daughters to dream on their own terms. By doing so, we raise the volume of their voices and give them the power to shape their futures.

Bonus: Resource Toolkit

———————⊰⊱⊰⊱———————

Navigating the world as a neurodivergent individual can be challenging, but with the right resources and support, the journey can become more manageable and empowering. This Resource Toolkit is designed to provide you with valuable tools, resources, and strategies to help neurodivergent girls (and their families) thrive. Whether you are seeking books for personal development, apps for organization and focus, websites for education and support, or communities for connection, this toolkit has something for everyone. Additionally, the conversation prompts, reflection worksheets, and printable planners will help you actively engage in the process of self-advocacy and personal growth.

1. Recommended Books, Apps, Websites, and Communities

Books

- **"NeuroTribes: The Legacy of Autism and the Future of Neurodiversity" by Steve Silberman**
  - A must-read for understanding the history of autism and neurodiversity. Silberman offers a comprehensive look at how the neurodiversity movement has shaped our understanding of autism and other neurodivergent conditions.

- **"The ADHD Advantage: What You Thought You Knew About ADHD May Be Wrong" by Dale Archer, M.D.**

- This book provides a positive, strengths-based perspective on ADHD, helping neurodivergent girls and their families appreciate the unique abilities that come with ADHD rather than focusing solely on the challenges.

- **"The Curious Incident of the Dog in the Night-Time" by Mark Haddon**

  - This fictional novel provides insight into the mind of a neurodivergent individual with autism, offering a glimpse into how a different perspective can shape the experience of the world. A great read for teens to understand others with similar experiences.

- **"The Power of Different: The Link Between Disorder and Genius" by Gail Saltz, M.D.**

  - Dr. Saltz explores how neurodivergent traits can often lead to innovation and success, helping to reframe how society views individuals with conditions like ADHD, autism, and dyslexia.

- **"Uniquely Human: A Different Way of Seeing Autism" by Barry M. Prizant**

  - A compassionate and insightful exploration of autism that focuses on the strengths and abilities of individuals with autism. It also provides practical advice for parents and caregivers on how to support neurodivergent individuals.

Apps

- **Todoist**

  - This task management app is ideal for neurodivergent girls who struggle with organization and time management. Todoist allows users to break down tasks into smaller steps and set reminders to stay on track. It's a helpful tool for promoting independence and organization.

- **Forest**
  - A productivity app that helps with focus and staying on task. Users "grow" a tree by staying off their phones and focusing on a task for a set period. It's a great way for neurodivergent girls to build focus without feeling overwhelmed.

- **MindMeister**
  - This mind-mapping app helps neurodivergent individuals organize their thoughts visually. It's great for brainstorming, planning, and breaking down complex tasks into manageable pieces.

- **Calm**
  - Calm is a meditation and mindfulness app that can help neurodivergent individuals manage anxiety, stress, and sensory overload. It includes guided meditations, sleep stories, and breathing exercises to support emotional regulation.

- **My Autism Team**
  - An online social network for families of children with autism. My Autism Team connects parents, caregivers, and individuals to share advice, resources, and experiences in a supportive community setting.

Websites

- **Autism Speaks (autismspeaks.org)**
  - Autism Speaks provides a wealth of information, resources, and advocacy tools for parents, caregivers, and individuals with autism. It includes educational content,

support groups, and access to research in the field of autism.

- **ADDitude (additudemag.com)**
  - A comprehensive online resource dedicated to ADHD, ADDitude offers advice, strategies, and expert articles on managing ADHD in all aspects of life—from education to relationships to careers.

- **Neurodiversity.com**
  - This site offers resources for families, educators, and neurodivergent individuals. It includes articles, research, and personal stories that help people embrace neurodiversity in all its forms.

- **Understood (understood.org)**
  - A valuable resource for parents and educators of neurodivergent children. Understood provides tips, strategies, and tools for managing ADHD, dyslexia, and other learning differences. It also offers personalized resources based on specific needs.

- **The National Autistic Society (nas.org.uk)**
  - This UK-based organization provides resources for individuals with autism, their families, and professionals. It includes a wealth of information on autism, including advocacy, support services, and educational tools.

Communities

- **Reddit: r/ADHD, r/Autism, r/Neurodiversity**
  - These subreddits are full of individuals who share personal experiences, coping strategies, and resources related to ADHD, autism, and neurodiversity. They provide a platform for sharing stories and learning from others in similar situations.

- **Facebook Groups:**
  - There are several Facebook groups dedicated to supporting families of neurodivergent children. Some examples include "ADHD Parents Support Group," "Autism Moms," and "Neurodiversity Advocacy Group." These groups allow for connection, advice sharing, and mutual support.
- **The Neurodiversity Movement (neurodiversitymovement.com)**
  - An online community that supports and advocates for neurodivergent individuals, emphasizing acceptance and the value of neurodiversity in society. It includes resources, advocacy tools, and educational content.

2. Conversation Prompts and Reflection Worksheets

Conversation Prompts for Parents and Daughters:

- **What do you love most about how your brain works?**
  - This question encourages your daughter to reflect on her strengths and how neurodivergence can be an asset.
- **What do you find most challenging in school/work/social situations?**
  - This prompt helps identify areas where your daughter might need additional support or accommodations.
- **If you could change one thing about the world to make it more accessible for people like you, what would it be?**
  - This allows your daughter to think about larger societal changes and express her desires for inclusivity.
- **What would an ideal day look like for you, without any limitations?**

- Encourages visioning the future and understanding what makes her happiest and most fulfilled.

- **When was the last time you felt proud of yourself? Why?**

  - A question that highlights positive moments and helps build self-esteem.

Reflection Worksheets:

1. **My Neurodivergent Strengths**

   - List five strengths or qualities that make you proud of your neurodivergent brain.

   - How do these strengths help you in school, work, or relationships?

   - Reflect on how you can continue to develop these strengths in the future.

2. **Challenges and Coping Strategies**

   - Write down three challenges you face regularly (e.g., social situations, focus, organization).

   - What strategies have you used in the past to manage these challenges?

   - What new strategies can you try to improve your coping?

3. **My Vision for the Future**

   - What do you want your life to look like in 5 years? 10 years?

   - What are your goals for school, work, and relationships?

   - How can you take small steps today to move closer to those goals?

4. **Advocacy in Action**

   - Describe a time when you advocated for yourself (e.g., asking for accommodations, expressing your needs).

○ How did it feel to speak up for yourself?

○ What are three new ways you can advocate for yourself in the future?

3. Printable Planner or Checklist for Parents

Neurodivergent Girls' Self-Advocacy Planner

Use this planner to track your daughter's progress in building self-advocacy skills, identifying areas where she may need support, and creating goals for growth. This tool also helps parents stay organized and provide targeted support.

Date	Goal	Action Steps	Support Needed	Progress/Reflection
[Insert Date]	Advocate for a classroom accommodation	1. Discuss needs with teacher	Parent to help outline accommodations	[Insert notes on success or challenges]
[Insert Date]	Learn how to ask for sensory breaks	1. Practice script for asking	Parent to help role-play situations	[Insert notes on how it felt]
[Insert Date]	Explore a new social group	1. Identify a group based on interest	Parent to research group options	[Insert thoughts on participation]
[Insert Date]	Develop a time management plan	1. Break tasks into steps	Parent to assist in creating the plan	[Insert reflections on effectiveness]

Parent Reflection Checklist

Item	Yes/No		Notes	
Have I allowed my daughter to express her needs?	[ ] Yes		[ ] No	
Do I model self-advocacy in my own life?	[ ] Yes		[ ] No	
Have we discussed neurodivergence and its strengths?	[ ] Yes		[ ] No	
Have I celebrated my daughter's progress recently?	[ ] Yes		[ ] No	
Am I setting aside time for self-care and support?	[ ] Yes		[ ] No	

Conclusion

This Resource Toolkit is designed to provide parents, caregivers, and neurodivergent girls with the tools and strategies needed to navigate the challenges of self-advocacy, self-discovery, and empowerment. From books that reframe the narrative around neurodivergence to apps that help with focus and productivity, these resources are intended to support a journey of growth, learning, and connection. By using the conversation prompts, reflection worksheets, and printable planners, both parents and daughters can embark on a journey of self-awareness, self-advocacy, and a deeper understanding of what it means to live authentically and with pride.

www.ingramcontent.com/pod-product-compliance
Lightning Source LLC
Chambersburg PA
CBHW070127030426
42335CB00016B/2290

*9 7 8 1 9 6 9 7 0 3 2 9 4 *